Learn Selenium in 1 Day

By Krishna Rungta

Table of Content

Chapter 1: Introduction to Selenium

What is Selenium?

Selenium is a free (open source) automated testing suite for web applications across different browsers and platforms. It is quite similar to HP Quick Test Pro (QTP now UFT) only that Selenium focuses on automating web-based applications. Testing done using Selenium tool is usually referred as Selenium Testing.

Selenium is not just a single tool but a suite of software's, each catering to different testing needs of an organization. **It has four components.**

- Selenium Integrated Development Environment (IDE)

- Selenium Remote Control (RC)

- WebDriver

- Selenium Grid

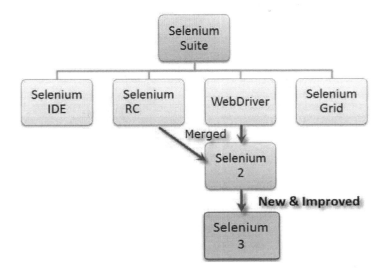

At the moment, Selenium RC and WebDriver are merged into a single framework to form **Selenium 2**. Selenium 1, by the way, refers to Selenium RC.

Who developed Selenium?

Since Selenium is a collection of different tools, it had different developers as well. Below are the key persons who made notable contributions to the Selenium Project

Primarily, Selenium was **created by Jason Huggins in 2004**. An engineer at ThoughtWorks, he was working on a web application that required frequent testing. Having realized that the repetitious manual testing of their application was becoming more and more inefficient, he created a **JavaScript** program that would automatically control the browser's actions. He named this program as the **"JavaScriptTestRunner."**

Seeing potential in this idea to help automate other web applications, he made JavaScriptRunner open-source which was later re-named as **Selenium Core**.

The Same Origin Policy Issue

Same Origin policy prohibits JavaScript code from accessing elements from a domain that is different from where it was launched. Example, the HTML code in www.google.com uses a JavaScript program "randomScript.js". The same origin policy will only allow randomScript.js to access pages within google.com such as google.com/mail, google.com/login, or google.com/signup. However, it cannot access pages from different sites such as yahoo.com/search or guru99.com because they belong to different domains.

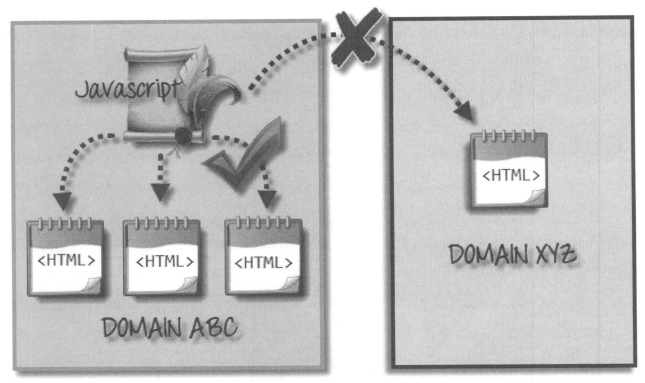

under same origin policy, a javascript program can only access pages on the same domain where it belongs. It cannot access pages from different domains

This is the reason why prior to Selenium RC, testers needed to install local copies of both Selenium Core (a JavaScript program) and the web server containing the web application being tested so they would belong to the same domain

Birth of Selenium Remote Control (Selenium RC)

Paul Hammant

Unfortunately; testers using Selenium Core had to install the whole application under test and the web server on their own local computers because of the restrictions imposed by the **same origin policy.** So another ThoughtWork's engineer, **Paul Hammant**, decided to create a server that will act as an HTTP proxy to "trick" the browser into believing that Selenium Core and the web application being tested come from the same domain. This system became known as the **Selenium Remote Control** or **Selenium 1**.

Birth of Selenium Grid

Patrick Lightbody

Selenium Grid was developed by **Patrick Lightbody** to address the need of minimizing test execution times as much as possible. He initially called the system **"Hosted QA."** It was capable of capturing browser screenshots during significant stages, and also of **sending out Selenium commands to different machines simultaneously.**

Birth of Selenium IDE

Shinya Kasatani of Japan created **Selenium IDE**, a Firefox extension that can automate the browser through a record-and-playback feature. He came up with this idea to further increase the speed in creating test cases. He donated Selenium IDE to the Selenium Project in **2006**.

Birth of WebDriver

Simon Stewart

Simon Stewart created WebDriver circa **2006** when browsers and web applications were becoming more powerful and more restrictive with JavaScript programs like Selenium Core. **It was the first cross-platform testing framework that could control the browser from the OS level.**

Birth of Selenium 2

In **2008**, the whole Selenium Team decided to merge WebDriver and Selenium RC to form a more powerful tool called **Selenium 2**, with **WebDriver being the core**. Currently, Selenium RC is still being developed but only in maintenance mode. Most of the Selenium Project's efforts are now focused on Selenium 2.

So, Why the Name Selenium?

It came from a joke which Jason cracked one time to his team. Another automated testing framework was popular during Selenium's development, and it was by the company called **Mercury Interactive** (yes, the company who originally made QTP before it was acquired by HP). Since Selenium is a well-known antidote for Mercury poisoning, Jason suggested that name. His teammates took it, and so that is how we got to call this framework up to the present.

Brief Introduction Selenium IDE

Selenium Integrated Development Environment (IDE) is the **simplest framework** in the Selenium suite and is **the easiest one to learn**. It is a **Firefox plugin** that you can install as easily as you can with other plugins. However, because of its simplicity, Selenium IDE should only be used as a **prototyping tool**. If you want to create more advanced test cases, you will need to use either Selenium RC or WebDriver.

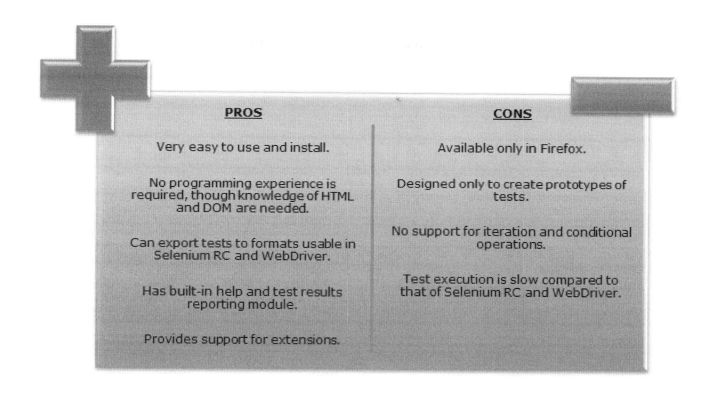

PROS	CONS
Very easy to use and install.	Available only in Firefox.
No programming experience is required, though knowledge of HTML and DOM are needed.	Designed only to create prototypes of tests.
Can export tests to formats usable in Selenium RC and WebDriver.	No support for iteration and conditional operations.
Has built-in help and test results reporting module.	Test execution is slow compared to that of Selenium RC and WebDriver.
Provides support for extensions.	

Brief Introduction Selenium Remote Control (Selenium RC)

Selenium RC was the **flagship testing framework** of the whole Selenium project for a long time. This is the first automated web testing tool that **allowed users to use a programming language they prefer**. As of version 2.25.0, RC can support the following programming languages:

- **Java**

- **C#**

- **PHP**

- Python

- Perl

- Ruby

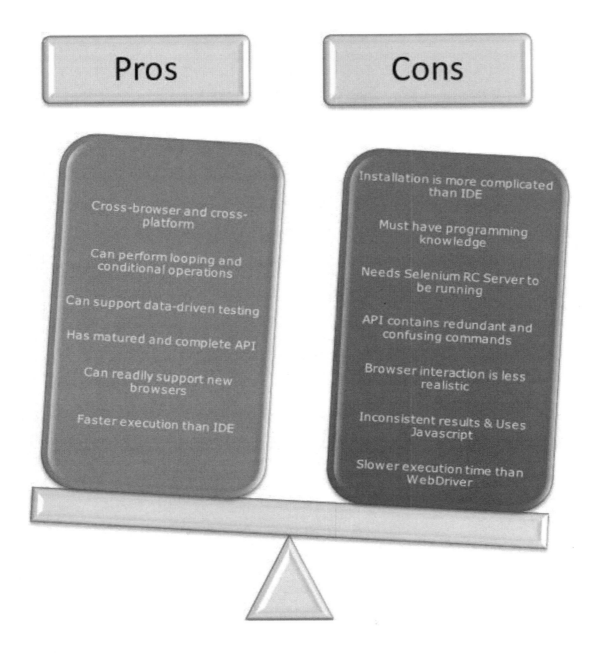

Brief Introduction WebDriver

The WebDriver proves itself to be **better than both Selenium IDE and Selenium RC** in many aspects. It implements a more modern and stable approach in automating the browser's actions. WebDriver, unlike Selenium RC, does not rely on JavaScript for Automation. **It controls the browser by directly communicating with it.**

The supported languages are the same as those in Selenium RC.

- Java
- C#
- PHP

- Python
- Perl
- Ruby

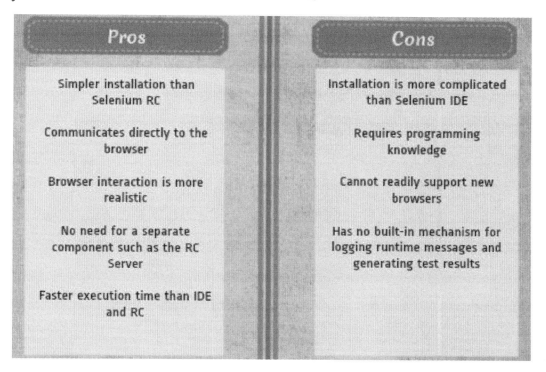

Selenium Grid

Selenium Grid is a tool **used together with Selenium RC to run parallel tests** across different machines and different browsers all at the same time. Parallel execution means running multiple tests at once.

Features:

- Enables **simultaneous running of tests** in **multiple browsers and environments.**
- **Saves time** enormously.
- Utilizes the **hub-and-nodes** concept. The hub acts as a central source of Selenium commands to each node connected to it.

Note on Browser and Environment Support

Because of their architectural differences, Selenium IDE, Selenium RC, and WebDriver support different sets of browsers and operating environments.

	Selenium IDE	WebDriver

	Selenium IDE	WebDriver
BrowserSupport	Mozilla Firefox	Internet Explorer versions 6 to 11, both 32 and 64-bit Microsoft Edge version 12.10240 & above (partial support some functionalities under development) Firefox 3.0 and above Google Chrome 12.0. and above Opera 11.5 and above Android - 2.3 and above for phones and tablets (devices & emulators) iOS 3+ for phones (devices & emulators) and 3.2+ for tablets (devices & emulators) HtmlUnit 2.9 and above
Operating System	Windows, Mac OS X, Linux	All operating systems where the browsers above can run.

Note: Selenium WebDriver is termed as the successor of Selenium RC which has been deprecated & officially announced by SeleniumHQ.

How to Choose the Right Selenium Tool for Your Need

Tool	Why Choose?
Selenium IDE	<ul><li>To learn about concepts on automated testing and Selenium, including:<ul><li>Selenese commands such as type, open, clickAndWait, assert, verify, etc.</li><li>Locators such as id, name, xpath, css selector, etc.</li><li>Executing customized JavaScript code using runScript</li><li>Exporting test cases in various formats.</li></ul></li><li>To create tests with little or no prior knowledge in programming.</li><li>To create simple test cases and test suites that you can</li></ul>

Tool	Why Choose?
	export later to RC or WebDriver. • To test a web application against Firefox only.
Selenium RC	• To design a test using a more expressive language than Selenese • To run your test against different browsers (except HtmlUnit) on different operating systems. • To deploy your tests across multiple environments using Selenium Grid. • To test your application against a new browser that supports JavaScript. • To test web applications with complex AJAX-based scenarios.
WebDriver	• To use a certain programming language in designing your test case. • To test applications that are rich in AJAX-based functionalities. • To execute tests on the HtmlUnit browser. • To create customized test results.
Selenium Grid	• To run your Selenium RC scripts in multiple browsers and operating systems simultaneously. • To run a huge test suite, that needs to complete in the soonest time possible.

A Comparison between Selenium and QTP(now UFT)

Quick Test Professional(QTP) is a proprietary automated testing tool previously owned by the company **Mercury Interactive** before it was **acquired by Hewlett-Packard in 2006**. The Selenium Tool Suite has many advantages over QTP as detailed below -

Advantages of Selenium over QTP

Selenium	QTP
Open source, **free to use**, and **free of charge.**	**Commercial**.
Highly extensible	Limited add-ons
Can run tests across **different browsers**	Can only run tests in **Firefox**, **Internet Explorer** and **Chrome**
Supports **various operating systems**	Can only be used in **Windows**
Supports **mobile devices**	QTP Supports Mobile app test automation (iOS & Android) using HP solution called - HP Mobile Center
Can execute tests **while** the **browser is minimized**	Needs to have the application under test to be visible on the desktop
Can execute tests **in parallel**.	Can only execute in parallel but using Quality Center which is again a paid product.

Advantages of QTP over Selenium

QTP	Selenium
Can test **both web and desktop applications**	Can only test web applications
Comes with a **built-in object repository**	Has no built-in object repository
Automates faster than Selenium because it is a fully featured IDE.	Automates at a slower rate because it does not have a native IDE and only third party IDE can be used for development
Data-driven testing is easier to perform because **it has built-in global and local**	Data-driven testing is more cumbersome since you have to rely on the programming

data tables.	language's capabilities for setting values for your test data
Can access controls within the browser(such as the Favorites bar, Address bar, Back and Forward buttons, etc.)	Cannot access elements outside of the web application under test
Provides professional **customer support**	No official user support is being offered.
Has native capability to **export test data** into external formats	Has no native capability to export runtime data onto external formats
Parameterization Support is built	Parameterization can be done via programming but is difficult to implement.
Test Reports are generated automatically	No native support to generate test /bug reports.

Though clearly, **QTP** has more advanced capabilities, Selenium outweighs QTP in three main areas:

- **Cost**(because Selenium is completely free)

- **Flexibility**(because of a number of programming languages, browsers, and platforms it can support)

- **Parallel testing**(something that QTP is capable of but only with use of Quality Center)

Summary

- The entire Selenium Tool Suite is comprised of four components:

    - **Selenium IDE**, a Firefox add-on that you can only use in creating relatively simple test cases and test suites.

- **Selenium Remote Control**, also known as **Selenium 1**, which is the first Selenium tool that allowed users to use programming languages in creating complex tests.

- **WebDriver**, the newer breakthrough that allows your test scripts to communicate directly to the browser, thereby controlling it from the OS level.

- **Selenium Grid** is also a tool that is used with Selenium RC to execute parallel tests across different browsers and operating systems.

- Selenium RC and WebDriver was merged to form **Selenium 2**.

- Selenium is more advantageous than QTP in terms of **costs and flexibility**. It also allows you to **run tests in parallel**, unlike in QTP where you are only allowed to run tests sequentially.

Chapter 2: Install Selenium IDE and FireBug

Installation of Selenium IDE

What you need

- Mozilla Firefox

- Active Internet Connection

If you do not have Mozilla Firefox yet, you can download it from **http://www.mozilla.org/en-US/firefox/new**.

Selenium IDE Works with all major versions, but we recommend to use 47.0.1 & above as they have better stability.

Steps 1)

Launch Firefox and navigate to **https://addons.mozilla.org/en-US/firefox/addon/selenium-ide/**. Click on Add to Firefox

Steps 2)

Wait until Firefox completes the download and then click "**Install.**"

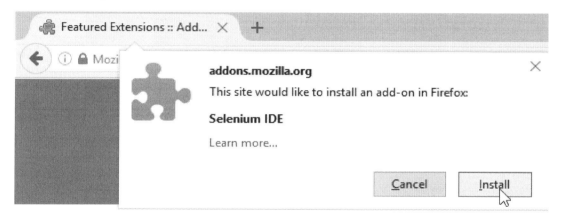

Steps 3)

Wait until the installation is completed. In the pop-up window, click "**Restart Now**."

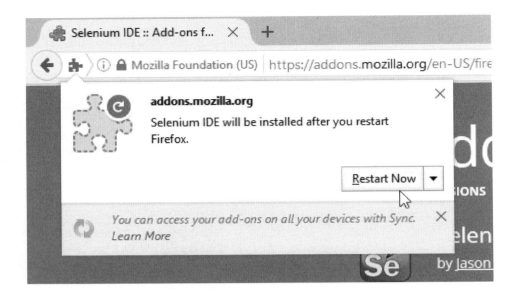

Steps 4)

After Firefox has restarted, **launch Selenium IDE** using either of two ways:

- By pressing **Ctrl+Alt+S**
- By clicking on the **Firefox menu button**> **Developer**>**Selenium IDE**

Steps 5)

Selenium IDE should launch as shown below

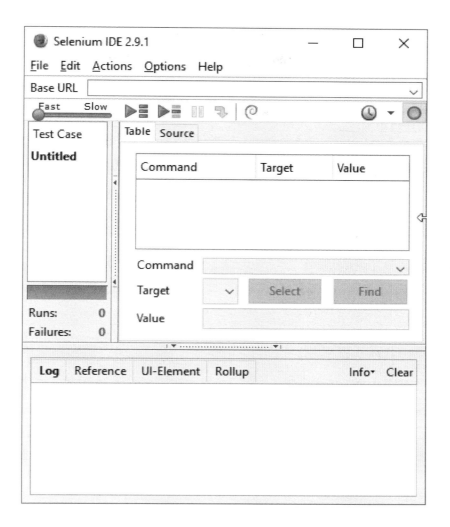

Installation of Firebug

Firebug is a Firefox add-on that we will use to **inspect the HTML elements** of the web application under test. It will provide us the name of the element that our Selenese command would act upon.

Step 1

Use Firefox to navigate to Firebug's download page (**https://addons.mozilla.org/en-US/firefox/addon/firebug/**) and click on the download link.

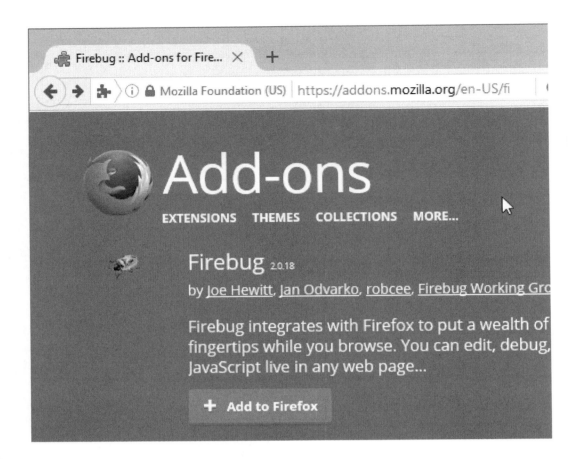

Step 2

Wait for Firefox to complete downloading this add-on. On the dialog box that comes after, click **"Install Now."**

Step 3

Wait for the installation to complete. A notification will pop-up saying, "Firebug has been installed successfully." You can immediately close this pop-up.

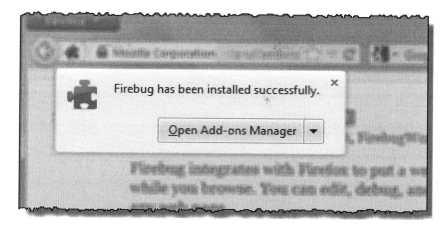

Note: In case if you do not see above pop-up, no worries! This pop-up appears for a few seconds and disappears.

You do not need to restart Firefox after installing Firebug.

Step 4

Launch Firebug by doing either of these two methods:

- Press **F12**

- Click on the **Firebug button** in the upper right corner of the Firefox window.

Step 5

Firebug should launch **at the bottom of Firefox** as shown below

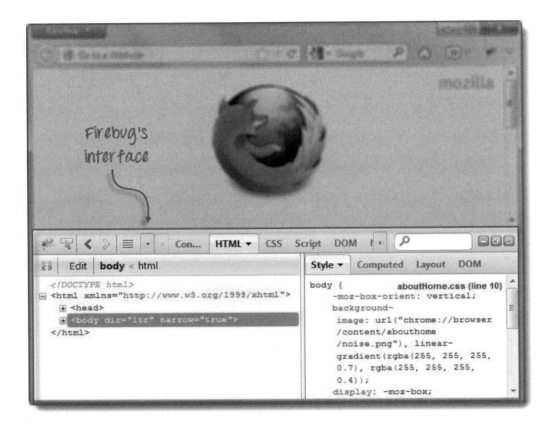

Note: Firebug Extension is no longer under development and is deprecated as mentioned on firebug's site

The Firebug extension isn't being developed or maintained any longer. We invite you to use the **Firefox DevTools** instead, which ship with Firebug.next

See also Migration from Firebug guide.

We Recommend using Firefox DevTools

You can access Firefox DevTools by using following steps

- Open Firefox
- Press Ctrl + Shift + "I"

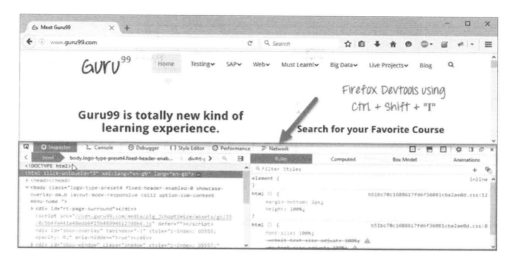

Note: Advantage of using Firebug over DevTools is that, in FireBug, you can directly copy the XPath of a WebElement to be used in Selenium. Hence we use it in our tutorials

Plugins

Selenium IDE can support additional Firefox add-ons or plugins created by other users. You can visit **here** for a list of Selenium add-ons available to date. Install them just as you do with other Firefox add-ons.

By default, Selenium IDE comes bundled with 4 plugins:

1. Selenium IDE: **C#** Formatters

2. Selenium IDE: **Java** Formatters

3. Selenium IDE: **Python** Formatters

4. Selenium IDE: Ruby Formatters

These four plugins are required by Selenium IDE to convert Selenese into different formats.

The Plugins tab shows a list of all your installed add-ons, together with the version number and name of the creator of each.

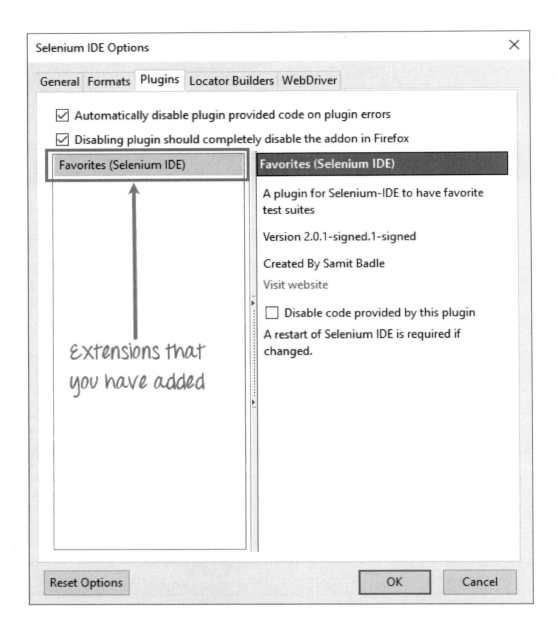

User Extensions

Selenium IDE can support user extensions to provide advanced capabilities. User extensions are in the form of **JavaScript** files. You install them by specifying their absolute path in either of these two fields in the Options dialog box.

- Selenium Core extensions (user-extensions.js)
- Selenium IDE extensions

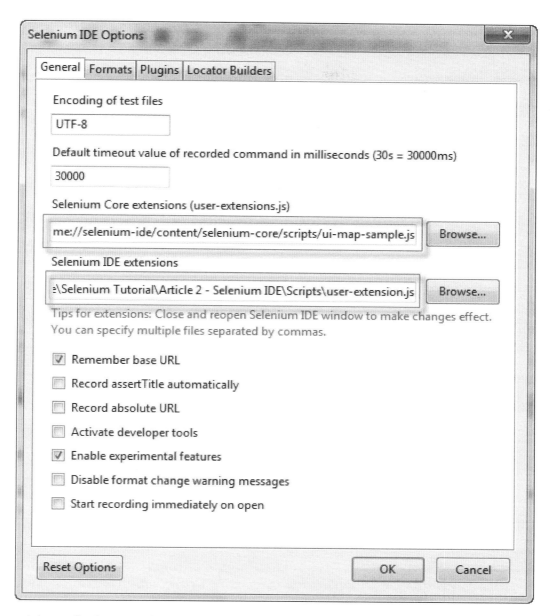

You will be able to find tons of user extensions **here.**

Chapter 3: Introduction to Selenium IDE

Selenium IDE (Integrated Development Environment) is the simplest tool in the Selenium Suite. It is a Firefox add-on that creates tests very quickly through its record-and-playback functionality. This feature is similar to that of QTP. It is effortless to install and easy to learn.

Because of its simplicity, Selenium IDE should only be used as a prototyping tool, not an overall solution for developing and maintaining complex test suites.

Though you will be able to use Selenium IDE without prior knowledge in programming, you should at least be familiar with HTML, JavaScript, and the DOM (Document Object Model) to utilize this tool to its full potential. Knowledge of **JavaScript** will be required when we get to the section about the Selenese command **"runScript."**

Selenium IDE supports autocomplete mode when creating tests. This feature serves two purposes:

- It helps the tester to enter commands more quickly.

- It restricts the user from entering invalid commands.

Features of Selenium IDE

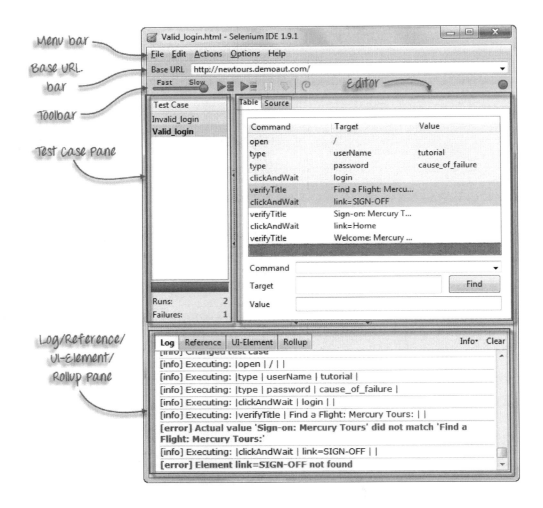

Menu Bar

It is located at the **top most portion** of the IDE. The most commonly used menus are the File, Edit, and Options menus.

File menu

- It contains options to create, open, save and close tests.

- Tests are **saved in HTML format**.

- The most useful option is **"Export"** because **it allows you to turn your Selenium IDE test cases into file formats that can run on Selenium Remote Control and WebDriver**

  - **"Export Test Case As..."** will export only the currently opened test case.

  - **"Export Test Suite As..."** will export all the test cases in the currently opened test suite.

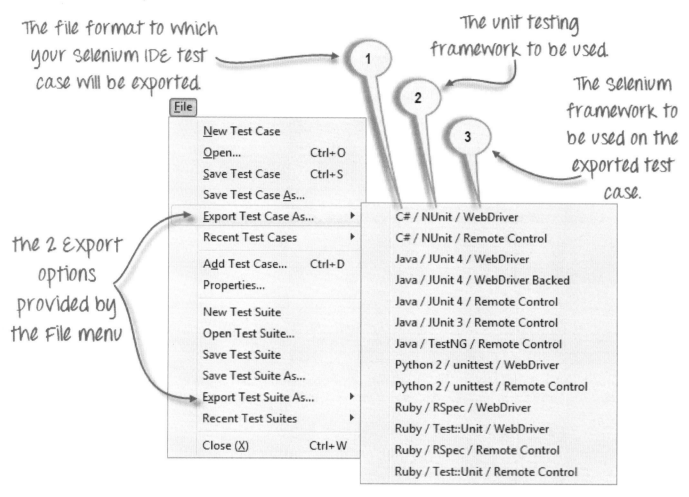

- As of **Selenium IDE v1.9.1**, test cases can be exported only to the following formats:

- .cs (C# source code)

- .java (Java source code)

- .py (Python source code)

- .rb (Ruby source code)

selenium IDE test case   WebDriver test case

Edit Menu

- It contains usual options like Undo, Redo, Cut, Copy, Paste, Delete, and Select All.

- The two most important options are the **"Insert New Command"** and **"Insert New Comment"**.

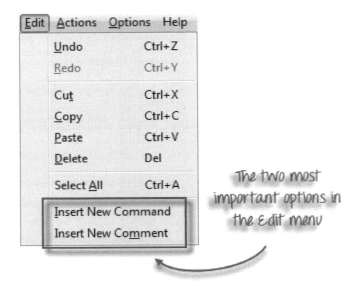

The two most important options in the Edit menu

- The newly inserted command or comment **will be placed on top of the currently selected line**.

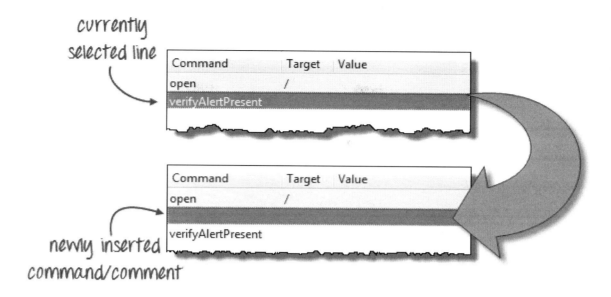

currently selected line

newly inserted command/comment

- **Commands** are colored **black**.
- **Comments** are colored **purple.**

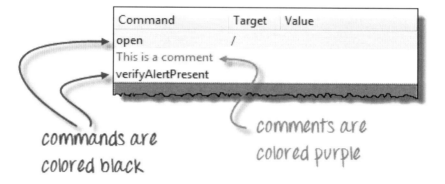

commands are colored black

comments are colored purple

Options menu

It provides the **interface for configuring various settings** of Selenium IDE.

We shall concentrate on the **Options** and **Clipboard Format** options.

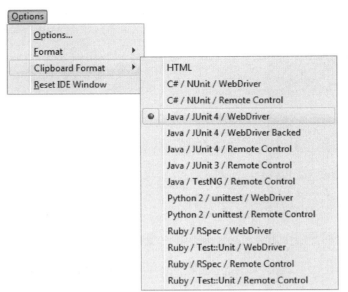

Clipboard Format

- **The Clipboard Format allows you to copy a Selenese command from the editor and paste it as a code snippet**.

- The format of the code follows the option you selected here in Clipboard Format's list.

- **HTML is the default selection.**

For example, when you choose **Java/JUnit 4/WebDriver** as your clipboard format, every Selenese command you copy from Selenium IDE's editor will be pasted as **Java code**. See the illustration below.

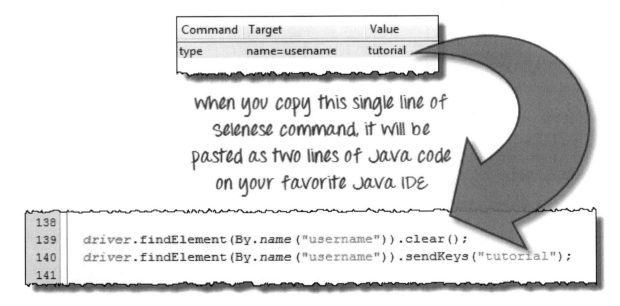

Selenium IDE Options dialog box

You can launch the Selenium IDE Options dialog box by clicking Options > Options... on the menu bar. Though there are many settings available, we will concentrate on the few important ones.

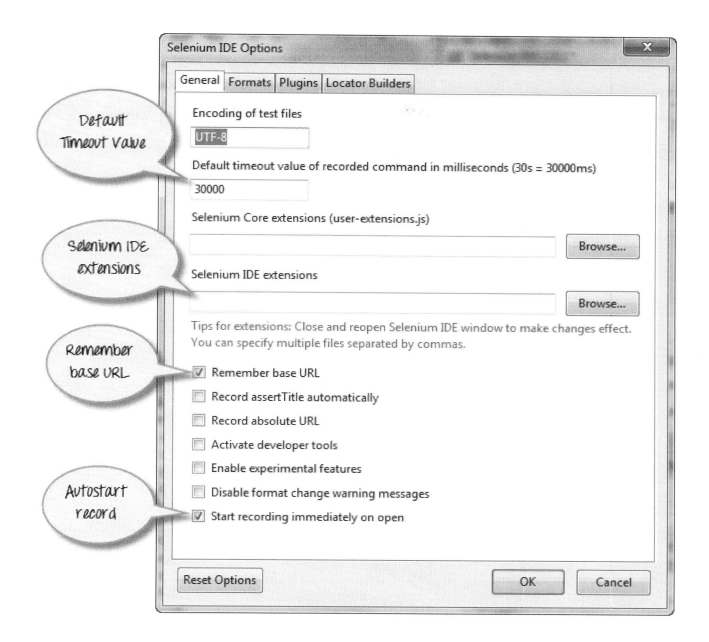

- **Default Timeout Value**. This refers to the time that Selenium has to wait for a certain element to appear or become accessible before it generates an error. **Default timeout value is 30000ms**.

- **Selenium IDE extensions**. This is where you specify the extensions you want to use to extend Selenium IDE's capabilities. You can visit **http://addons.mozilla.org/en-US/firefox/** and use "Selenium" as a keyword to search for the specific extensions.

- **Remember base URL.** Keep this checked if you want Selenium IDE to remember the Base URL every time you launch it. If you uncheck this, Selenium IDE will always launch with a blank value for the Base URL.

- **Autostart record.** If you check this, Selenium IDE will immediately record your browser actions upon startup.

- **Locator builders.** This is where you specify the order by which locators are generated while recording. **Locators are ways to tell Selenium IDE which UI element should a Selenese command act upon**. In the setup below, when you click on an element with an ID attribute, that element's ID will be used as the locator since "id" is the first one in the list. If that element does not have an ID attribute, Selenium will next look for the "name" attribute since it is second in the list. The list goes on and on until an appropriate one is found.

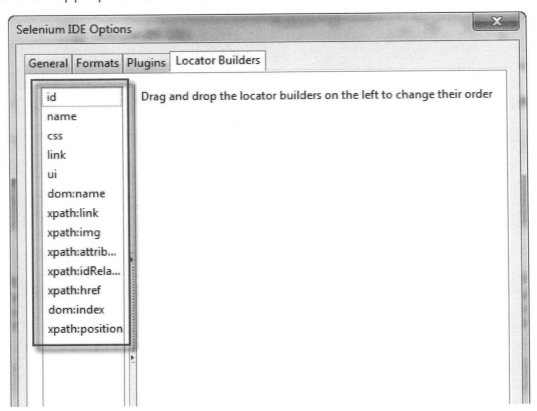

Base URL Bar

- It has **a dropdown menu that remembers all previous values** for easy access.

- The Selenese command **"open" will take you to the URL that you specified in the Base URL**.

- In this tutorial series, we will be using **http://newtours.demoaut.com** as our Base URL. It is the site for Mercury Tours, a web application maintained by HP for web **Testing** purposes. We shall be using this application because it contains a complete set of elements that we need for the succeeding topics.

- **The Base URL is very useful in accessing relative URLs**. Suppose that your Base URL is set to **http://newtours.demoaut.com**. When you execute the command "open" with the target value "signup," Selenium IDE will direct the browser to the sign-up page. See the illustration below.

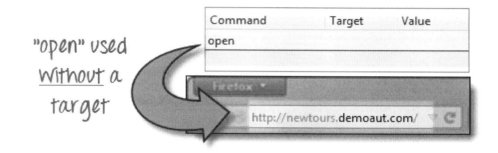

"open" used
Without a
target

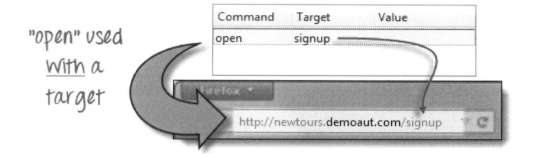

"open" used
With a
target

Toolbar

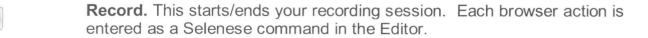

Playback Speed. This controls the speed of your Test Script Execution.

Record. This starts/ends your recording session. Each browser action is entered as a Selenese command in the Editor.

Play entire test suite. This will sequentially play all the test cases listed in the Test Case Pane.

 Play current test case. This will play only the currently selected test case in the Test Case Pane.

 Pause/Resume. This will pause or resume your playback.

 Step. This button will allow you to step into each command in your test script.

 Apply rollup rules. This is an advanced functionality. It allows you to group Selenese commands together and execute them as a single action.

Test Case Pane

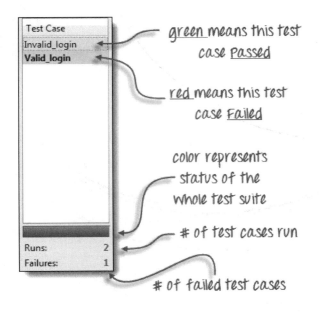

- In Selenium IDE, you can open **more than one test case at a time**.

- **The test case pane shows you the list of currently opened test cases.**

- When you open a test suite, the test case pane will **automatically list all the test cases** contained in it.

- The test case written in **bold font** is the **currently selected test case**

- After playback, **each test case is color-coded** to represent if it passed or failed.

  - Green color means "Passed."

  - Red color means "Failed."

- At the bottom portion is a summary of the number of test cases that were run and failed.

Editor

You can think of the editor as **the place where all the action happens**. It is available in two views: Table and Source.

Table View

- Most of the time, you will work on Selenium IDE using the **Table View**.

- This is **where you create and modify Selenese commands.**

- After playback, each step is color-coded.

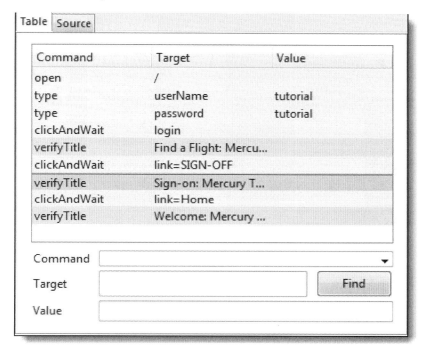

- To create steps, type the name of the command in the "Command" text box.

- **It displays a dropdown list of commands** that match with the entry that you are currently typing.

- Target is any parameter (like username, password) for a command and Value is the input value (like tom, 123pass) for those Targets.

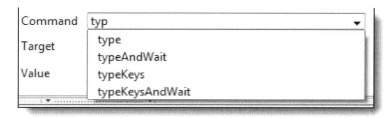

Source View

- It displays the steps in HTML (default) format.

- It also allows you to edit your script just like in the Table View.

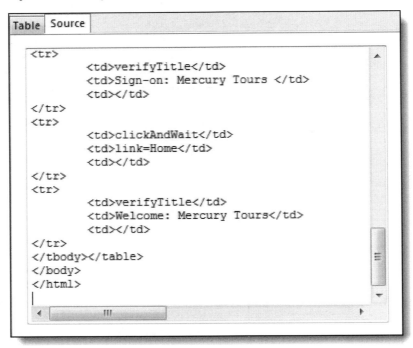

Log Pane

The Log Pane displays runtime messages during execution. It provides real-time updates as to what Selenium IDE is doing.

Logs are categorized into four types:

- Debug - By default, Debug messages are not displayed in the log panel. They show up only when you filter them. They provide technical information about what Selenium IDE is doing behind the scenes. It may display messages such as a specific module has done loading, a certain function is called, or an external JavaScript file was loaded as an extension.

- Info - It says which command Selenium IDE is currently executing.

- Warn - These are warning messages that are encountered in special situations.

- Error - These are error messages generated when Selenium IDE fails to execute a command, or if a condition specified by "verify" or "assert" command is not met.

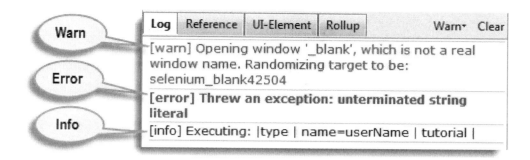

Logs can be filtered by type. For example, if you choose to select the "Error" option from the dropdown list, the Log Pane will show error messages only.

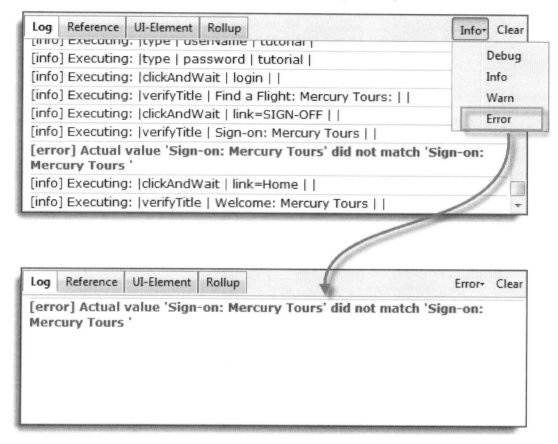

Reference Pane

The Reference Pane shows a concise description of the currently selected Selenese command in the Editor. It also shows the **description about the locator and value** to be used on that command.

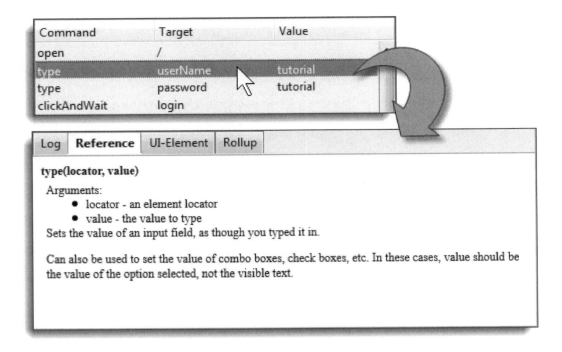

UI-Element Pane

The UI-Element is for advanced Selenium users. **It uses JavaScript Object Notation (JSON) to define element mappings.** The documentation and resources are found in the "UI Element Documentation" option under the Help menu of Selenium IDE.

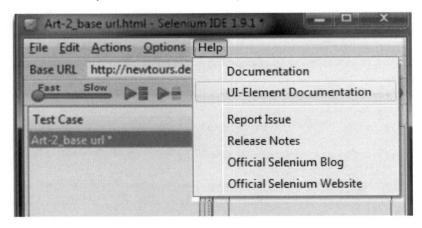

An example of a UI-element screen is shown below.

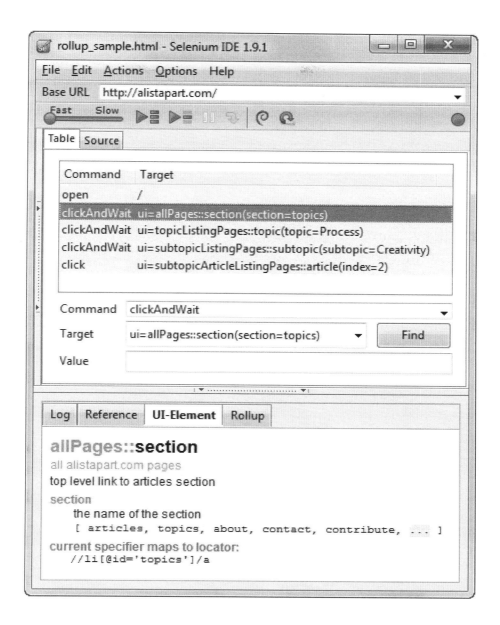

Rollup Pane

Rollup allows you to execute a group of commands in one step. A group of commands is simply called as a "rollup." It employs heavy use of JavaScript and UI-Element concepts to formulate a collection of commands that is similar to a "function" in programming languages.

Rollups are reusable; meaning, they can be used multiple times within the test case. Since rollups are groups of commands condensed into one, they contribute a lot in shortening your test script.

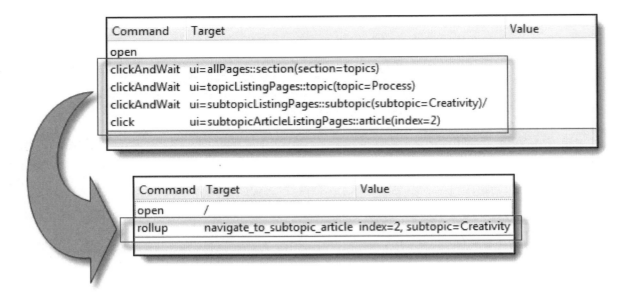

An example of how the contents of the rollup tab look like is shown below.

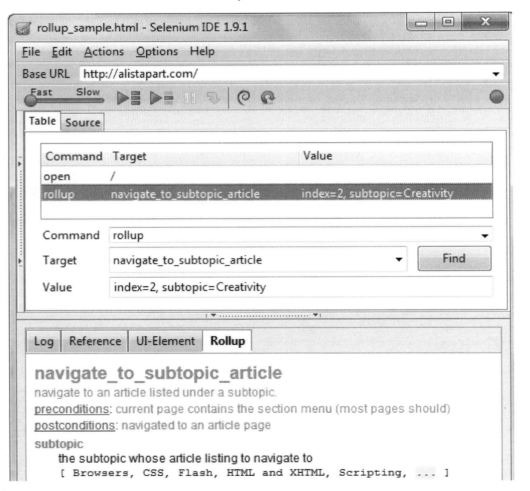

Summary

- Selenium IDE (Integrated Development Environment) **is the simplest tool** in the Selenium Suite.

- It must only be used as a **prototyping tool**.

- **Knowledge of JavaScript and HTML is required for intermediate topics** such as executing the "runScript" and "rollup" commands. A **rollup** is a collection of commands that you can reuse to shorten your test scripts significantly. **Locators** are identifiers that tell Selenium IDE how to access an element.

- **Firebug** (or any similar add-on) is used to obtain locator values.

- The **menu bar** is used in creating, modifying, and exporting test cases into formats useable by Selenium RC and WebDriver.

- The **default format for Selenese commands is HTML**.

- The **"Options" menu provides access to various configurations** for Selenium IDE.

- The **Base URL** is useful in accessing **relative URLs**.

- The **Test Case Pane** shows the list of currently opened test cases and a concise summary of test runs.

- The **Editor** provides the **interface for your test scripts**.

- The **Table View** shows your script **in tabular format** with "Command", "Target", and "Value" as the columns.

- The **Source View** shows your script **in HTML format**.

- The **Log** and **Reference** tabs give feedback and other useful information when executing tests.

- The **UI-Element and Rollup** tabs are **for advanced Selenium IDE users only**. They both require considerable effort in coding JavaScript.

- **UI-Element** allows you to **conveniently map UI elements** using JavaScript Object Notation (JSON).

The following table summarizes the release history for the Selenium IDE.

Major version	Release date
1.0.10	06-Dec-10
1.5.0	15-Dec-11
1.8.1	01-Jun-12
2.1.0	30-Jun-13
2.2.0	06-Jul-13
2.3.0	09-Aug-13
2.5.0	02-Jan-14
2.8.0	29-Sep-14
2.9.0	09-Mar-15
2.9.1	- to be released

Chapter 4: Creating your First Selenium IDE script

We will use the Mercury Tours website as our web application under test. It is an online flight reservation system that contains all the elements we need for this tutorial. Its URL is **http://newtours.demoaut.com/**, and this will be our Base URL.

Create a Script by Recording

Let us now create our first test script in Selenium IDE using the most common method - by recording. Afterward, we shall execute our script using the playback feature.

Step 1

- Launch Firefox and Selenium IDE.

- Type the value for our Base URL: **http://newtours.demoaut.com/**.

- Toggle the Record button on (if it is not yet toggled on by default).

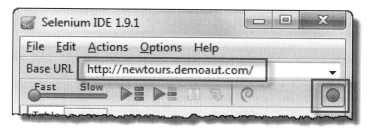

Step 2

In Firefox, navigate to **http://newtours.demoaut.com/**. Firefox should take you to the page similar to the one shown below.

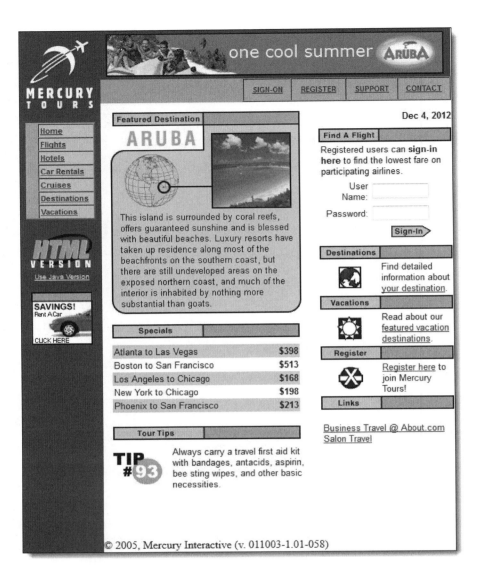

Step 3

- Right-click on any blank space within the page, like on the Mercury Tours logo on the
- upper left corner. This will bring up the Selenium IDE context menu. Note:
- Do not click on any hyperlinked objects or images
- Select the "Show Available Commands" option.
- Then, select "assertTitle exact: Welcome: Mercury Tours."

  This is a command that makes

  Sure that the page title is correct.

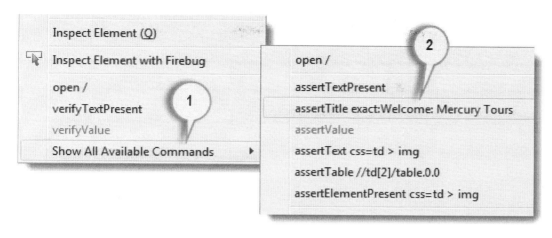

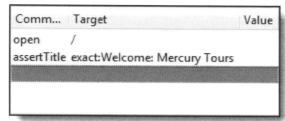

Comm...	Target	Value
open	/	
assertTitle	exact:Welcome: Mercury Tours	

After clicking on the assertTitle
context menu option, your Selenium
IDE Editor pane should now contain
the following commands

Step 4

- In the "User Name" text box of Mercury Tours, type an invalid username, "invalidUNN".

- In the "Password" text box, type an invalid password, "invalidPWD".

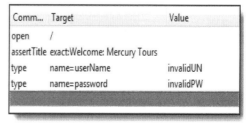

Comm...	Target	Value
open	/	
assertTitle	exact:Welcome: Mercury Tours	
type	name=userName	invalidUN
type	name=password	invalidPW

Your Editor should now look like this

Step 5

- Click on the "Sign-In" button. Firefox should take you to this page.

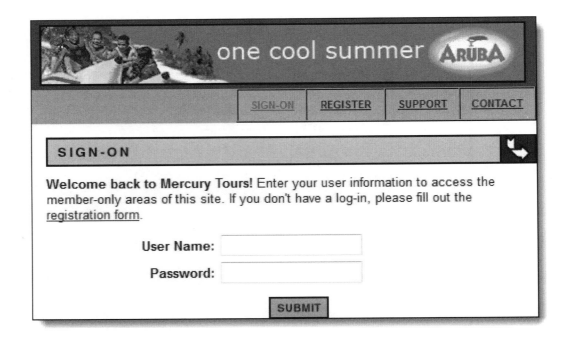

Step 6

Toggle the record button off to stop recording. Your script should now look like the one shown below.

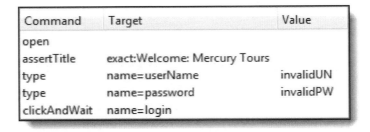

Command	Target	Value
open		
assertTitle	exact:Welcome: Mercury Tours	
type	name=userName	invalidUN
type	name=password	invalidPW
clickAndWait	name=login	

Step 7

Now that we are done with our test script, we shall save it in a test case. In the File menu, select "Save Test Case". Alternatively, you can simply press Ctrl+S.

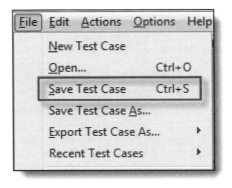

Step 8

- Choose your desired location, and then name the test case as "Invalid_login".

- Click the "Save" button.

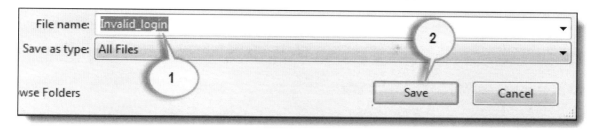

Step 9.

Notice that the file was saved as HTML.

Step 10.

Go back to Selenium IDE and click the Playback button to execute the whole script. Selenium IDE should be able to replicate everything flawlessly.

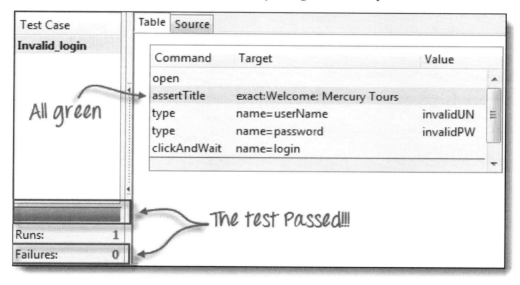

Introduction to Selenium Commands - Selenese

- Selenese commands can have up to a maximum of two parameters: target and value.

- Parameters are not required all the time. It depends on how many the command will need.

- For a complete reference of Selenese commands

3 Types of Commands

Actions	These are commands that directly interact with page elements. Example: the "click" command is an action because you directly interact with the element you are clicking at. The "type" command is also an action because you are putting values into a text box, and the text box shows them to you in return. There is a two-way interaction between you and the text box.
Accessors	They are commands that allow you to store values to a variable. Example: the "storeTitle" command is an accessor because it only "reads" the page title and saves it in a variable. It does not interact with any element on the page.

Assertions	They are commands that verify if a certain condition is met.
	
	 3 Types of Assertions
	
	 • **Assert**. When an "assert" command fails, the test is stopped immediately.
	
	 • **Verify**. When a "verify" command fails, Selenium IDE logs this failure and continues with the test execution.
	
	 • **WaitFor**. Before proceeding to the next command, "waitFor" commands will first wait for a certain condition to become true.
	
	      ○ If the condition becomes true within the waiting period, the step passes.
	
	      ○ If the condition does not become true, the step fails. Failure is logged, and test execution proceeds to the next command.
	
	      ○ By default, the timeout value is set to 30 seconds. You can change this in the Selenium IDE Options dialog under the

	General tab.

Assert vs. Verify

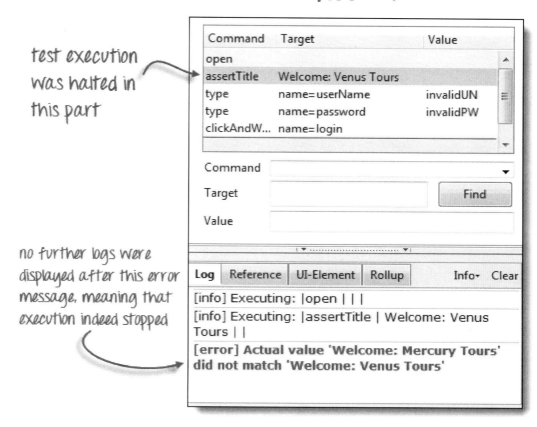

ASSERT

test execution was halted in this part

no further logs were displayed after this error message, meaning that execution indeed stopped

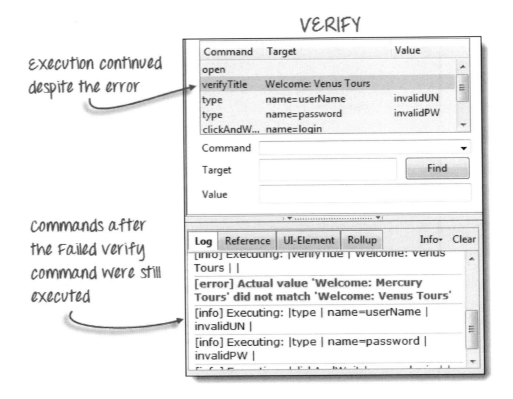

VERIFY

Execution continued despite the error

commands after the failed verify command were still executed

Common Commands

Command	Number of Parameters	Description
open	0 - 2	Opens a page using a URL.
click/clickAndWait	1	Clicks on a specified element.
type/typeKeys	2	Types a sequence of characters.
verifyTitle/assertTitle	1	Compares the actual page title with an expected value.
verifyTextPresent	1	Checks if a certain text is found within the page.
verifyElementPresent	1	Checks the presence of a certain element.

verifyTable	2	Compares the contents of a table with expected values.
waitForPageToLoad	1	Pauses execution until the page is loaded completely.
waitForElementPresent	1	Pauses execution until the specified element becomes present.

Create a Script Manually with Firebug

Now, we shall recreate the same test case manually, by typing in the commands. This time, we will need to use Firebug.

Step 1

- Open Firefox and Selenium IDE.

- Type the base URL (**http://newtours.demoaut.com/**).

- The record button should be OFF.

Step 2

Click on the topmost blank line in the Editor.

Type "open" in the Command text box and press Enter.

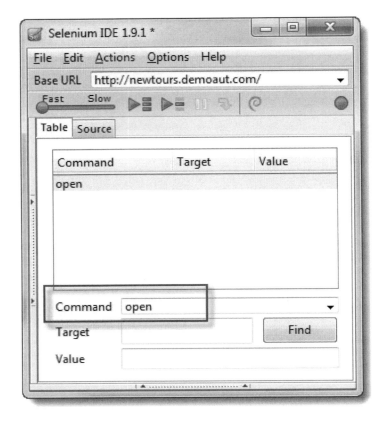

Step 3

- Navigate Firefox to our base URL and activate Firebug
- In the Selenium IDE Editor pane, select the second line
  (the line below the "open" command) and create the second command by typing
  "assertTitle" on the Command box.
- Feel free to use the autocomplete feature.

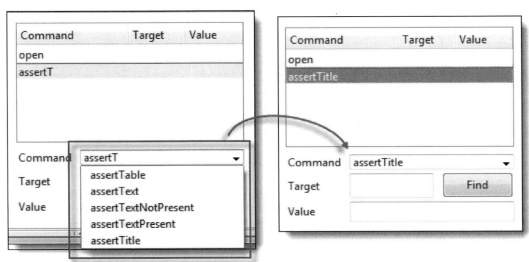

Step 4

- In Firebug, expand the <head> tag to display the <title> tag.

- Click on the value of the <title> tag (which is "Welcome: Mercury Tours") and paste it onto the Target field in the Editor.

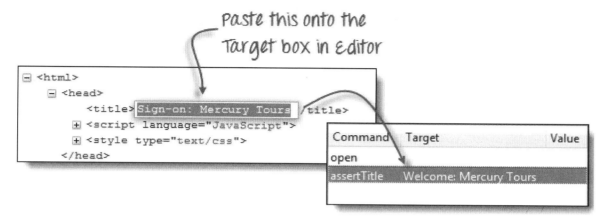

Step 5

- To create the third command, click on the third blank line in the Editor and key-in "type" on the Command text box.

- In Firebug, click on the "Inspect" button.

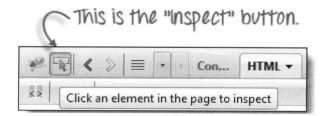

Click on the User Name text box. Notice that Firebug automatically shows you the HTML code for that element.

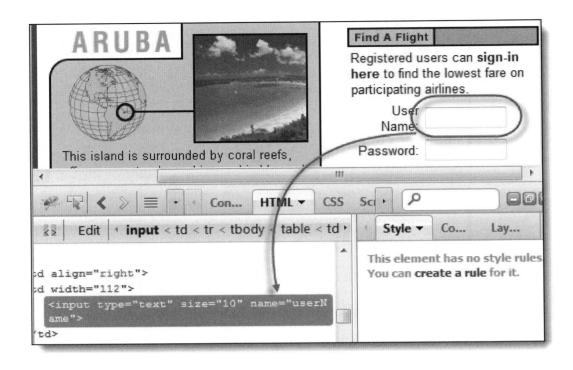

Step 6

Notice that the User Name text box does not have an ID, but it has a NAME attribute.

We shall, therefore, use its NAME as the locator. Copy the NAME value and paste it onto the Target field in Selenium IDE.

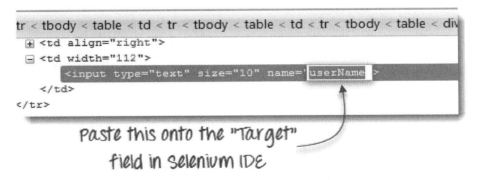

Paste this onto the "Target" field in Selenium IDE

Still in the Target text box, prefix "userName" with "name=", indicating that Selenium IDE should target an element whose NAME attribute is "userName."

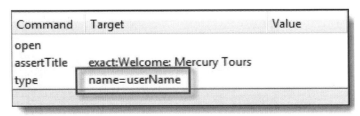

Type "invalidUN" in the Value text box of Selenium IDE. Your test script should now look like the image below. We are done with the third command. Note: Instead of invalidUN, you may enter any other text string. But Selenium IDE is case sensitive, and you type values/attributes exactly like in the application.

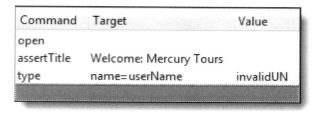

Command	Target	Value
open		
assertTitle	Welcome: Mercury Tours	
type	name=userName	invalidUN

Step 7

- To create the fourth command, key-in "type" on the Command text box.
- Again, use Firebug's "Inspect" button to get the locator for the "Password" text box.

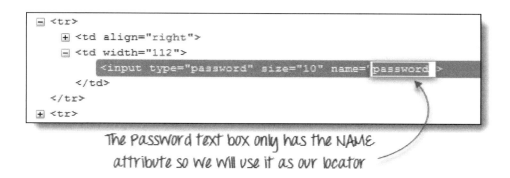

The Password text box only has the NAME attribute so we will use it as our locator

- Paste the NAME attribute ("password") onto the Target field and prefix it with "name="
- Type "invalidPW" in the Value field in Selenium IDE. Your test script should now look like the image below.

Step 8

- For the fifth command, type "clickAndWait" on the Command text box in Selenium IDE.
- Use Firebug's "Inspect" button to get the locator for the "Sign In" button.

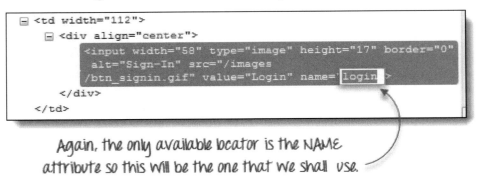

Again, the only available locator is the NAME attribute so this will be the one that we shall use.

- Paste the value of the NAME attribute ("login") onto the Target text box and prefix it with "name=".
- Your test script should now look like the image below.

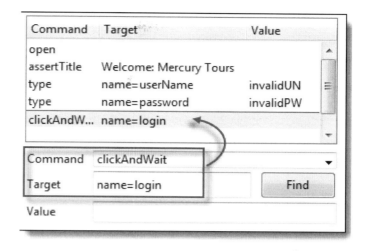

Step 9

Save the test case in the same way as we did in the previous section.

Using the Find Button

The Find button in Selenium IDE is used to verify if what we had put in the Target text box is indeed the correct UI element.

Let us use the Invalid_login test case that we created in the previous sections. Click on any command with a Target entry, say, the third command.

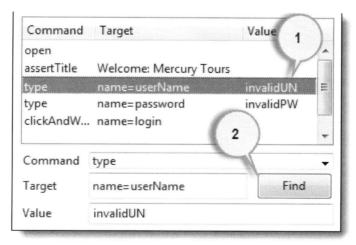

Click on the Find button. Notice that the User Name text box within the Mercury Tours page becomes highlighted for a second.

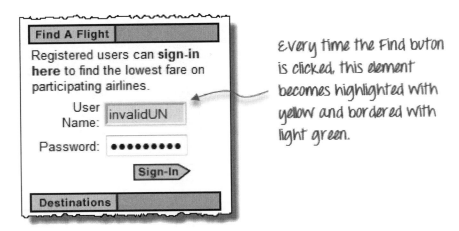

This indicates that Selenium IDE was able to detect and access the expected element correctly. If the Find button highlighted a different element or no element at all, then there must be something wrong with your script.

Execute Command

This allows you to execute any single command without running the whole test case. Just click on the line you wish to execute and then either click on "Actions > Execute this command" from the menu bar or simply press "X" on your keyboard.

Step 1. Make sure that your browser is on the Mercury Tours homepage.

Click on the command you wish to execute. In this example, click on the

"type | userName | invalidUN" line.

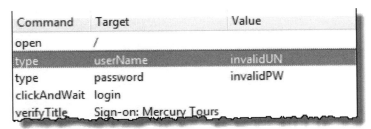

Step 2. Press "X" on your keyboard.

Step 3. Observe that the text box for username becomes populated with the text "invalidUN"

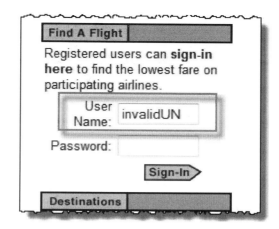

Executing commands this way is highly dependent on the page that Firefox is currently displaying. This means that if you try the example above with the Google homepage displayed instead of Mercury Tours', then your step will fail because there is no text box with a "userName" attribute within Google's homepage.

Start point

A start point is an indicator that tells Selenium IDE which lines the execution will start. Its shortcut key is "S".

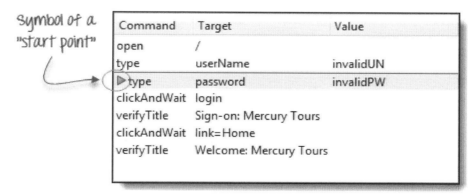

In the example above, playback will start on the third line (type | password | invalidPW). **You can only have one start point in a single test script.**

The start point is similar to Execute Command in such that they are dependent on the currently displayed page. The start point will fail if you are on the wrong page.

Breakpoints

Breakpoints are indicators that tell Selenium IDE where to automatically pause the test. **The shortcut key is "B".**

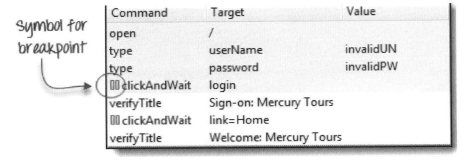

The yellow highlight means that the current step is pending. This proves that Selenium IDE has paused execution on that step. **You can have multiple breakpoints in one test case.**

Step

It allows you to execute succeeding commands one at a time after pausing the test case. Let us use the scenario in the previous section "Breakpoints."

Command	Target	Value
open	/	
type	userName	invalidUN
type	password	invalidPW
▥ clickAndWait	login	
verifyTitle	Sign-on: Mercury Tours	
▥ clickAndWait	link=Home	
verifyTitle	Welcome: Mercury Tours	

Before clicking "Step."

The test case pauses at the line "clickAndWait | login".

After clicking "Step."

The "clickAndWait | login" line is run and pauses to the next command (verifyTitle | Sign-on: Mercury Tours).

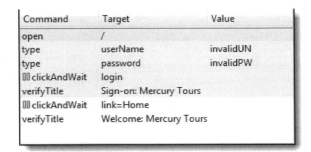

Notice that the next line is paused even though there is no breakpoint there. This is the main purpose of the Step feature - it executes the succeeding commands one at a time to give you more time to inspect the outcome after each step.

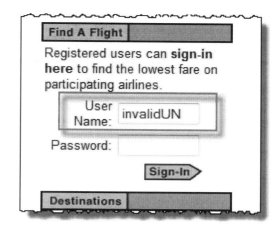

Executing commands this way is highly dependent on the page that Firefox is currently displaying. This means that if you try the example above with the Google homepage displayed instead of Mercury Tours', then your step will fail because there is no text box with a "userName" attribute within Google's homepage.

Start point

A start point is an indicator that tells Selenium IDE which lines the execution will start. Its shortcut key is "S".

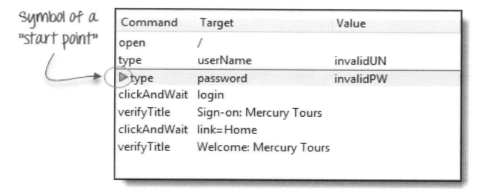

In the example above, playback will start on the third line (type | password | invalidPW). **You can only have one start point in a single test script.**

The start point is similar to Execute Command in such that they are dependent on the currently displayed page. The start point will fail if you are on the wrong page.

Breakpoints

Breakpoints are indicators that tell Selenium IDE where to automatically pause the test. **The shortcut key is "B".**

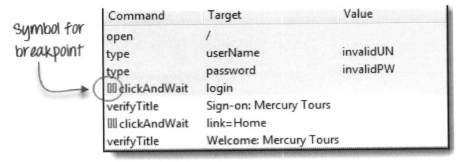

The yellow highlight means that the current step is pending. This proves that Selenium IDE has paused execution on that step. **You can have multiple breakpoints in one test case.**

Step

It allows you to execute succeeding commands one at a time after pausing the test case. Let us use the scenario in the previous section "Breakpoints."

Command	Target	Value
open	/	
type	userName	invalidUN
type	password	invalidPW
▯▯ clickAndWait	login	
verifyTitle	Sign-on: Mercury Tours	
▯▯ clickAndWait	link=Home	
verifyTitle	Welcome: Mercury Tours	

Before clicking "Step."

The test case pauses at the line "clickAndWait | login".

After clicking "Step."

The "clickAndWait | login" line is run and pauses to the next command (verifyTitle | Sign-on: Mercury Tours).

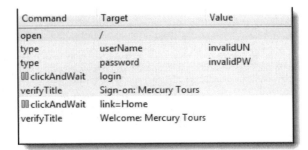

Notice that the next line is paused even though there is no breakpoint there. This is the main purpose of the Step feature - it executes the succeeding commands one at a time to give you more time to inspect the outcome after each step.

Important Things to Note When Using Other Formats in Source View

Selenium IDE works well only with HTML - other formats are still in experimental mode. It is **NOT advisable** to create or edit tests using other formats in Source View because there is still a lot of work needed to make it stable. Below are the known bugs as of version 1.9.1.

- You will not be able to perform playback nor switch back to Table View unless you revert to HTML.

- The only way to add commands safely on the source code is by recording them.

- When you modify the source code manually, all of it will be lost when you switch to another format.

- Though you can save your test case while in Source View, Selenium IDE will not be able to open it.

The recommended way to convert Selenese tests is to use the "Export Test Case As..." option under the File menu, and not through the Source View.

Summary

- Test scripts can be created either by recording or typing the commands and parameters manually.

- When creating scripts manually, Firebug is used to get the locator.

- The Find button is used to check that the command is able to access the correct element.

- Table View displays a test script in tabular form while Source View displays it in HTML format.

- Changing the Source View to a non-HTML format is still experimental.

- Do not use the Source View in creating tests in other formats. Use the Export features instead.

- Parameters are not required all the time. It depends upon the command.

- There are three types of commands:

    - Actions - directly interacts with page elements

    - Accessors - "reads" an element property and stores it in a variable

    - Assertions - compares an actual value with an expected one

- Assertions have three types:

    - Assert - upon failure, succeeding steps are no longer executed

    - Verify - upon failure, succeeding steps are still executed.

    - WaitFor - passes if the specified condition becomes true within the timeout period; otherwise, it will fail

- The most common commands are:

    - open

    - click/clickAndWait

    - type/typeKeys

    - verifyTitle/assertTitle

    - verifyTextPresent

    - verifyElementPresent

    - verifyTable

    - waitForPageToLoad

    - waitForElementPresent

Chapter 5: How to use Locators in Selenium IDE

What are Locators?

Locator is a command that tells Selenium IDE which GUI elements (say Text Box, Buttons, Check Boxes etc) its needs to operate on. Identification of correct GUI elements is a prerequisite to creating an automation script. But accurate identification of GUI elements is more difficult than it sounds. Sometimes, you end up working with incorrect GUI elements or no elements at all! Hence, Selenium provides a number of Locators to precisely locate a GUI element

The different types of Locators in Selenium IDE

- ID
- Name
- Link Text
- CSS Selector
    - Tag and ID
    - Tag and class
    - Tag and attribute
    - Tag, class, and attribute
    - Inner text
- DOM (Document Object Model)
    - getElementById
    - getElementsByName
    - dom:name
    - dom: index
- XPath

There are commands that do not need a locator (such as the "open" command). However, most of them do need Locators.

The choice of locator depends largely on your Application Under Test. In this tutorial, we will toggle between Facebook, new tours.demoaut on the basis of locators that these applications support. Likewise in your **Testing** project, you will select any of the above-listed locators based on your application support.

Locating by ID

This is the most common way of locating elements since ID's are supposed to be unique for each element.

Target Format: id=ID OF THE ELEMENT

For this example, we will use Facebook as our test app because Mercury Tours do not use ID attributes.

Step 1. Since this tutorial was created, Facebook has changed their Login Page Design. Use this demo page **http://demo.guru99.com/selenium/facebook.html** for testing. Inspect the "Email or Phone" text box using Firebug and take note of its ID. In this case, the ID is "email."

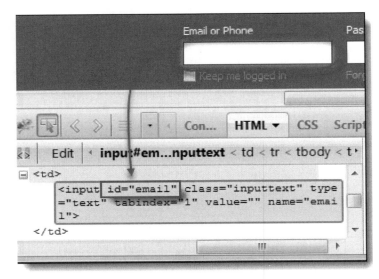

Step 2. Launch Selenium IDE and enter "id=email" in the Target box. Click the Find button and notice that the "Email or Phone" text box becomes highlighted with yellow and bordered with green, meaning, Selenium IDE was able to locate that element correctly.

Locating by Name

Locating elements by name are very similar to locating by ID, except that we use the **"name="** prefix instead.

Target Format: name=NAME OF THE ELEMENT

In the following demonstration, we will now use Mercury Tours because all significant elements have names.

Step 1. Navigate to **http://newtours.demoaut.com/** and use Firebug to inspect the "User Name" text box. Take note of its name attribute.

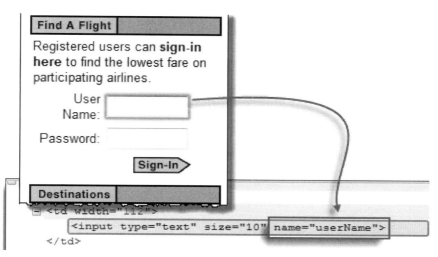

Here, we see that the element's name is "username".

Step 2. In Selenium IDE, enter "name=username" in the Target box and click the Find button. Selenium IDE should be able to locate the User Name text box by highlighting it.

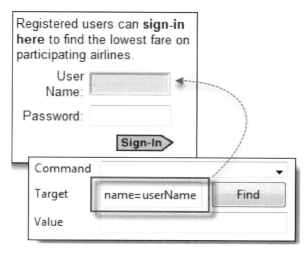

Locating by Name using Filters

Filters can be used when multiple elements have the same name. **Filters are additional attributes used to distinguish elements with the same name.**

Target Format: name=NAME_OF_THE_ELEMENT FILTER=VALUE_OF_FILTER

Let's see an example -

Step 1. Log on to Mercury Tours using "tutorial" as the username and password. It should take you to the Flight Finder page shown below.

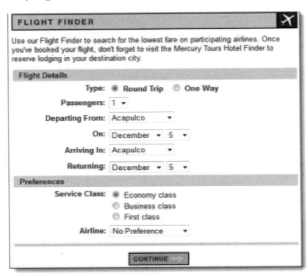

Step 2. Using Firebug, notice that the Round Trip and One Way radio buttons have the same name "tripType." However, they have different VALUE attributes so we can use each of them as our filter.

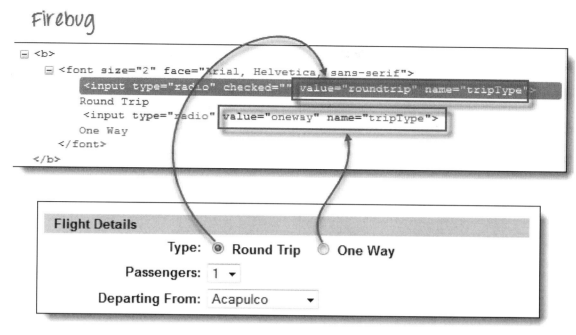

Firebug

Mercury Tours Flight Finder page

Step 3.

- We are going to access the One Way radio button first. Click the first line on the Editor.

- In the Command box of Selenium IDE, enter the command "click".

- In the Target box, enter "name=tripType value=oneway". The "value=oneway" portion is our filter.

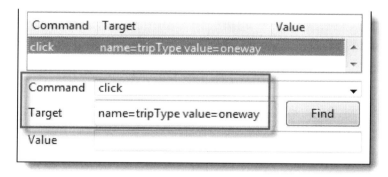

Step 4. Click the Find button and notice that Selenium IDE is able to highlight the One Way radio button with green - meaning that we are able to access the element successfully using its VALUE attribute.

Step 5. Press the "X" key in your keyboard to execute this click command. Notice that the One Way radio button became selected.

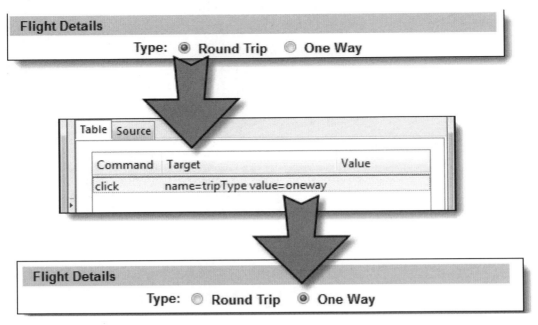

You can do the exact same thing with the Round Trip radio button, this time, using "name=tripType value=roundtrip" as your target.

Locating by Link Text

This type of locator applies only to hyperlink texts. We access the link by prefixing our target with "link=" and then followed by the hyperlink text.

Target Format: link=LINK_TEXT

In this example, we shall access the "REGISTER" link found on the Mercury Tours homepage.

Step 1.

- First, make sure that you are logged off from Mercury Tours.

- Go to Mercury Tours homepage.

Step 2.

- Using Firebug, inspect the "REGISTER" link. The link text is found between and tags.

- In this case, our link text is "REGISTER". Copy the link text.

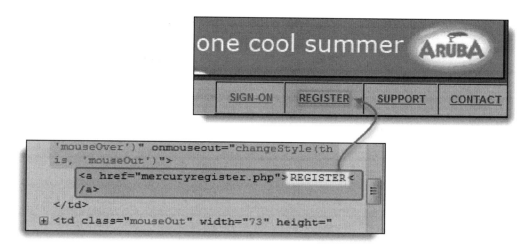

Step 3. Copy the link text in Firebug and paste it onto Selenium IDE's Target box. Prefix it with "link=".

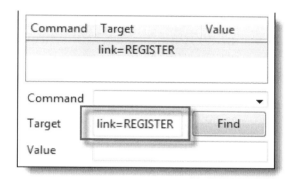

Step 4. Click on the Find button and notice that Selenium IDE was able to highlight the REGISTER link correctly.

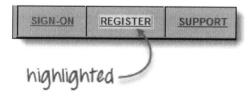

Step 5. To verify further, enter "clickAndWait" in the Command box and execute it. Selenium IDE should be able to click on that REGISTER link successfully and take you to the Registration page shown below.

REGISTER

To create your account, we'll need some basic information about you. This information will be used to send reservation confirmation emails, mail tickets when needed and contact you if your travel arrangements change. Please fill in the form completely.

Contact Information

First Name: _____

Last Name: _____

Phone: _____

Locating by CSS Selector

CSS Selectors are string patterns used to identify an element based on a combination of HTML tag, id, class, and attributes. Locating by CSS Selector is more complicated than the previous methods, but it is the most common locating strategy of advanced Selenium users because it can access even those elements that have no ID or name.

CSS Selectors have many formats, but we will only focus on the most common ones.

- Tag and ID

- Tag and class

- Tag and attribute

- Tag, class, and attribute

- Inner text

When using this strategy, we always prefix the Target box with "css=" as will be shown in the following examples.

Locating by CSS Selector - Tag and ID

Again, we will use Facebook's Email text box in this example. As you can remember, it has an ID of "email," and we have already accessed it in the "Locating by ID" section. This time, we will use a CSS Selector with ID in accessing that very same element.

Syntax	Description
css=TAG#ID	- tag = the HTML tag of the element being accessed

| | • # = the hash sign. This should always be present when using a CSS Selector with ID |
| | • id = the ID of the element being accessed |

Keep in mind that the ID is always preceded by a hash sign (#).

Step 1. Navigate to **www.facebook.com**. Using Firebug, examine the "Email or Phone" text box.

At this point, take note that the HTML tag is "input" and its ID is "email". So our syntax will be "css=input#email".

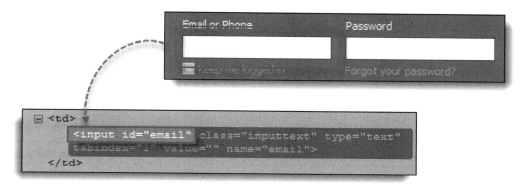

Step 2. Enter "css=input#email" into the Target box of Selenium IDE and click the Find button. Selenium IDE should be able to highlight that element.

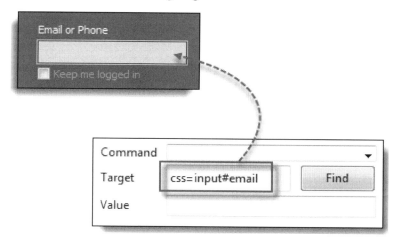

Locating by CSS Selector - Tag and Class

Locating by CSS Selector using an HTML tag and a class name is similar to using a tag and ID, but in this case, a dot (.) is used instead of a hash sign.

Syntax	Description
css=TAG.CLASS	<ul><li>tag = the HTML tag of the element being accessed</li><li>. = the dot sign. This should always be present when using a CSS Selector with class</li><li>class = the class of the element being accessed</li></ul>

Step 1. Go to the demo page **http://demo.guru99.com/selenium/facebook.html** and use Firebug to inspect the "Email or Phone" text box. Notice that its HTML tag is "input" and its class is "inputtext."

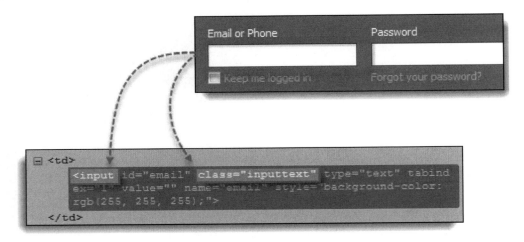

Step 2. In Selenium IDE, enter "css=input.inputtext" in the Target box and click Find. Selenium IDE should be able to recognize the Email or Phone text box.

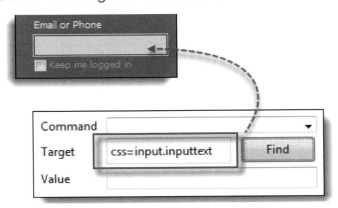

Take note that when multiple elements have the same HTML tag and name, only the first element in source code will be recognized. Using Firebug, inspect the Password text box in Facebook and notice that it has the same name as the Email or Phone text box.

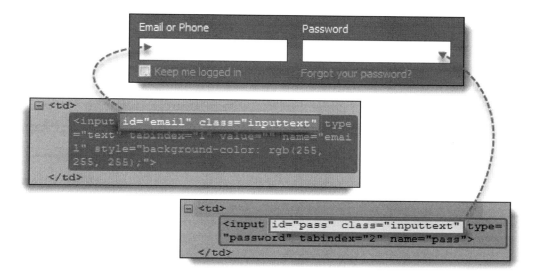

The reason why only the Email or Phone text box was highlighted in the previous illustration is that it comes first in Facebook's page source.

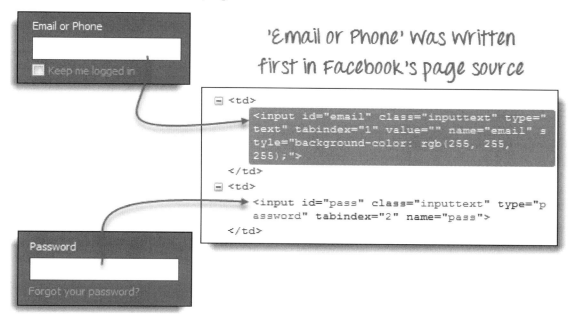

'Email or Phone' was written first in Facebook's page source

Locating by CSS Selector - Tag and Attribute

This strategy uses the HTML tag and a specific attribute of the element to be accessed.

Syntax	Description
css=TAG[ATTRIBUTE=VALUE]	• tag = the HTML tag of the element being accessed • [and] = square brackets within

	which a specific attribute and its corresponding value will be placed
	• attribute = the attribute to be used. It is advisable to use an attribute that is unique to the element such as a name or ID.
	• value = the corresponding value of the chosen attribute.

Step 1. Navigate to Mercury Tours' Registration page (**http://newtours.demoaut.com/mercuryregister.php**) and inspect the "Last Name" text box. Take note of its HTML tag ("input" in this case) and its name ("lastName").

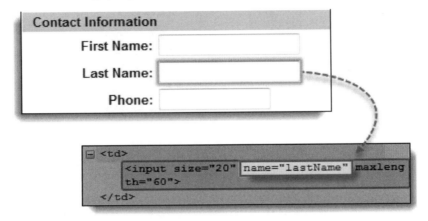

Step 2. In Selenium IDE, enter "css=input[name=lastName]" in the Target box and click Find. Selenium IDE should be able to access the Last Name box successfully.

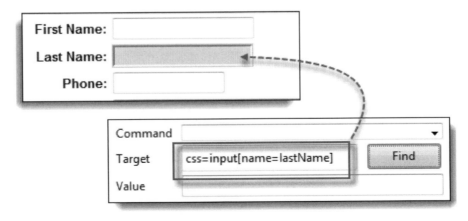

When multiple elements have the same HTML tag and attribute, only the first one will be recognized. This behavior is similar to locating elements using CSS selectors with the same tag and class.

Locating by CSS Selector - tag, class, and attribute

Syntax	Description
css=TAG.CLASS[ATTRIBUTE=VALUE]	• tag = the HTML tag of the element being accessed • . = the dot sign. This should always be present when using a CSS Selector with class • class = the class of the element being accessed • [and] = square brackets within which a specific attribute and its corresponding value will be placed • attribute = the attribute to be used. It is advisable to use an attribute that is unique to the element such as a name or ID. • value = the corresponding value of the chosen attribute.

Step 1. Go to the demo page **http://demo.guru99.com/selenium/facebook.html** and use Firebug to inspect the 'Email or Phone' and 'Password' input boxes. Take note of their HTML tag, class, and attributes. For this example, we will select their 'tabindex' attributes.

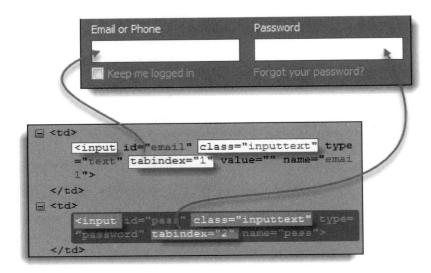

Step 2. We will access the 'Email or Phone' text box first. Thus, we will use a tabindex value of 1. Enter "css=input.inputtext[tabindex=1]" in Selenium IDE's Target box and click Find. The 'Email or Phone' input box should be highlighted.

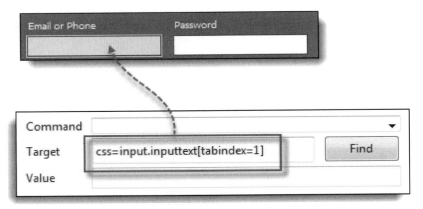

Step 3. To access the Password input box, simply replace the value of the tabindex attribute. Enter "css=input.inputtext[tabindex=2]" in the Target box and click on the Find button. Selenium IDE must be able to identify the Password text box successfully.

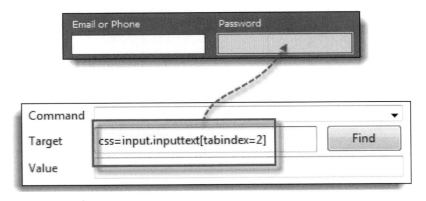

Locating by CSS Selector - inner text

As you may have noticed, HTML labels are seldom given id, name, or class attributes. So, how do we access them? The answer is through the use of their inner texts. **Inner texts are the actual string patterns that the HTML label shows on the page.**

Syntax	Description
css=TAG:contains("INNER TEXT")	• tag = the HTML tag of the element being accessed • inner text = the inner text of the element

Step 1. Navigate to Mercury Tours' homepage (**http://newtours.demoaut.com/**) and use Firebug to investigate the "Password" label. Take note of its HTML tag (which is "font" in this case) and notice that it has no class, id, or name attributes.

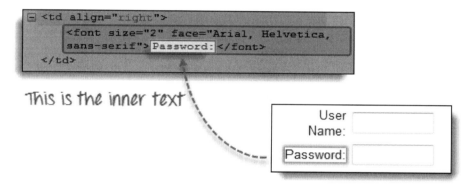

Step 2. Type **css=font:contains("Password:")** into Selenium IDE's Target box and click Find. Selenium IDE should be able to access the Password label as shown in the image below.

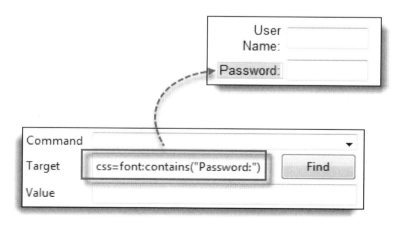

Step 3. This time, replace the inner text with "Boston" so that your Target will now become "css=font:contains("Boston")". Click Find. You should notice that the "Boston to San Francisco" label becomes highlighted. This shows you that Selenium IDE can access a long label even if you just indicated the first word of its inner text.

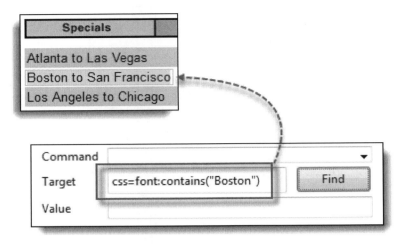

Locating by DOM (Document Object Model)

The Document Object Model (DOM), in simple terms, is the way by which HTML elements are structured. Selenium IDE is able to use the DOM in accessing page elements. If we use this method, our Target box will always start with "dom=document..."; however, the "dom=" prefix is normally removed because Selenium IDE is able to automatically interpret anything that starts with the keyword "document" to be a path within the DOM anyway.

There are four basic ways to locate an element through DOM:

- getElementById
- getElementsByName
- dom:name (applies only to elements within a named form)
- dom:index

Locating by DOM - getElementById

Let us focus on the first method - using the getElementById method. The syntax would be:

Syntax	Description
document.getElementById("ID OF THE ELEMENT")	id of the element = this is the value of the ID attribute of the element to be accessed. This value should always be enclosed in a pair of parentheses ("").

Step 1. Use this demo page **http://demo.guru99.com/selenium/facebook.html** Navigate to it and use Firebug to inspect the "Keep me logged in" check box. Take note of its ID.

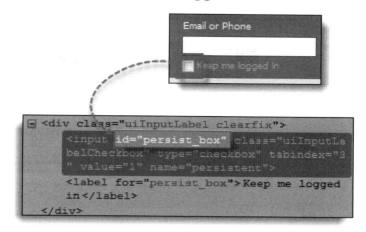

We can see that the ID we should use is "persist_box".

Step 2. Open Selenium IDE and in the Target box, enter "document.getElementById("persist_box")" and click Find. Selenium IDE should be able to locate the "Keep me logged in" check box. Though it cannot highlight the interior of the check box, Selenium IDE can still surround the element with a bright green border as shown below.

Locating by DOM - getElementsByName

The getElementById method can access only one element at a time, and that is the element with the ID that you specified. The getElementsByName method is different. It collects an array of elements that have the name that you specified. You access the individual elements using an index which starts at 0.

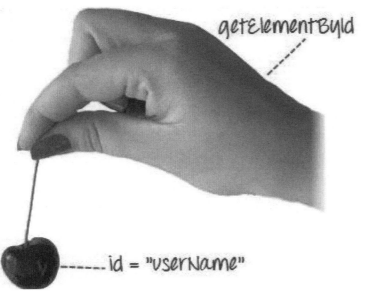

getElementById

- It will get only one element for you.

- That element bears the ID that you specified inside the parentheses of getElementById().

id = "userName"

getElementsByName

- It will get a collection of elements whose names are all the same.

- Each element is indexed with a number starting from 0 just like an array

- You specify which element you wish to access by putting its index number into the square brackets in getElementsByName's syntax below.

Syntax	Description

document.getElementsByName("NAME")[INDEX]	• name = name of the element as defined by its 'name' attribute
	• index = an integer that indicates which element within getElementsByName's array will be used.

Step 1. Navigate to Mercury Tours' Homepage and login using "tutorial" as the username and password. Firefox should take you to the Flight Finder screen.

Step 2. Using Firebug, inspect the three radio buttons at the bottom portion of the page (Economy class, Business class, and First class radio buttons). Notice that they all have the same name which is "servClass".

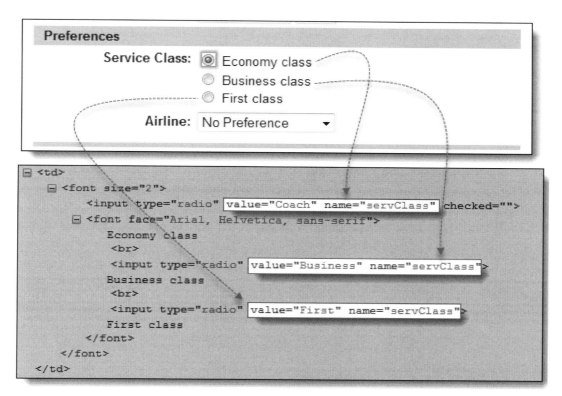

Step 3. Let us access the "Economy class" radio button first. Of all these three radio buttons, this element comes first, so it has an index of 0. In Selenium IDE, type "document.getElementsByName("servClass")[0]" and click the Find button. Selenium IDE should be able to identify the Economy class radio button correctly.

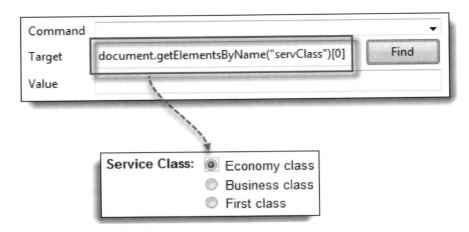

Step 4. Change the index number to 1 so that your Target will now become document.getElementsByName("servClass")[1]. Click the Find button, and Selenium IDE should be able to highlight the "Business class" radio button, as shown below.

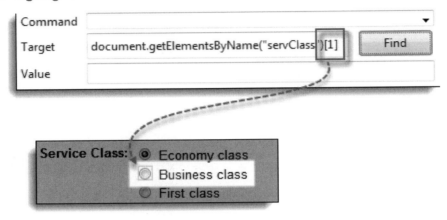

Locating by DOM - dom:name

As mentioned earlier, this method will only apply if the element you are accessing is contained within a named form.

Syntax	Description
document.forms["NAME OF THE FORM"].elements["NAME OF THE ELEMENT"]	• name of the form = the value of the name attribute of the form tag that contains the element you want to access • name of the element = the value of the name attribute of the element you wish to access

Step 1. Navigate to Mercury Tours homepage (**http://newtours.demoaut.com/**) and use Firebug to inspect the User Name text box. Notice that it is contained in a form named "home."

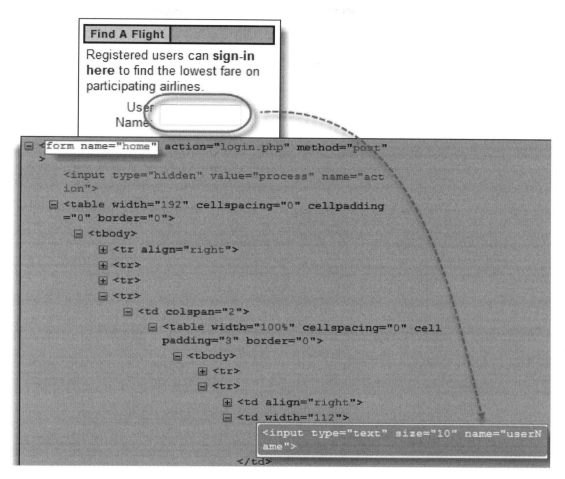

Step 2. In Selenium IDE, type "document.forms["home"].elements["userName"]" and click the Find button. Selenium IDE must be able to access the element successfully.

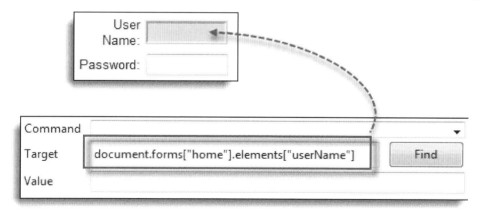

Locating by DOM - dom:index

This method applies even when the element is not within a named form because it uses the form's index and not its name.

Syntax	Description
document.forms[INDEX OF THE FORM].elements[INDEX OF THE ELEMENT]	• index of the form = the index number (starting at 0) of the form with respect to the whole page • index of the element = the index number (starting at 0) of the element with respect to the whole form that contains it

We shall access the "Phone" text box within Mercury Tours Registration page. The form in that page has no name and ID attribute, so this will make a good example.

Step 1. Navigate to Mercury Tours Registration page and inspect the Phone text box. Notice that the form containing it has no ID and name attributes.

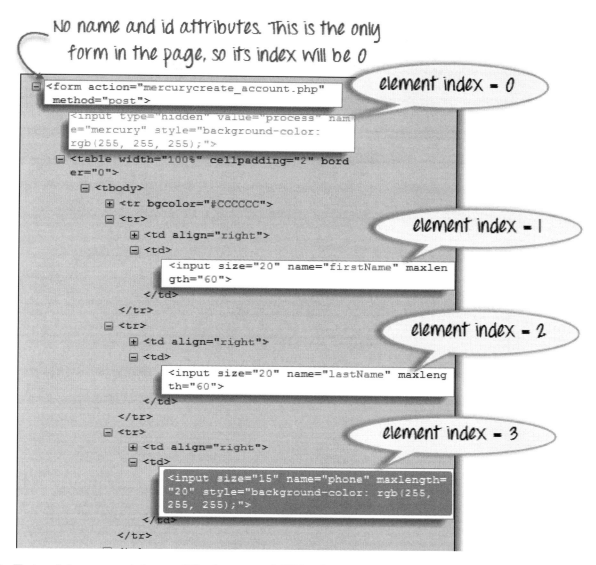

No name and id attributes. This is the only form in the page, so its index will be 0

element index - 0

element index - 1

element index - 2

element index - 3

Step 2. Enter "document.forms[0].elements[3]" in Selenium IDE's Target box and click the Find button. Selenium IDE should be able to access the Phone text box correctly.

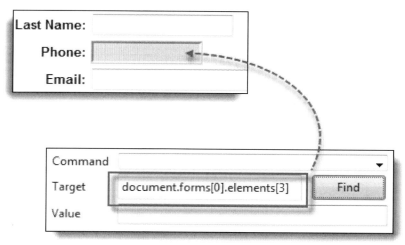

Step 3. Alternatively, you can use the element's name instead of its index and obtain the same result. Enter "document.forms[0].elements["phone"]" in Selenium IDE's Target box. The Phone text box should still become highlighted.

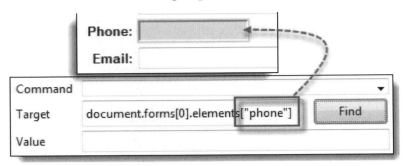

Locating by XPath

XPath is the language used when locating XML (Extensible Markup Language) nodes. Since HTML can be thought of as an implementation of XML, we can also use XPath in locating HTML elements.

     Advantage: It can access almost any element, even those without class, name, or id attributes.

     Disadvantage: It is the most complicated method of identifying elements because of too many different rules and considerations.

Fortunately, Firebug can automatically generate XPath locators. In the following example, we will access an image that cannot possibly be accessed through the methods we discussed earlier.

Step 1. Navigate to Mercury Tours Homepage and use Firebug to inspect the orange rectangle to the right of the yellow "Links" box. Refer to the image below.

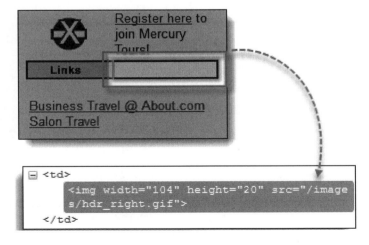

Step 2. Right click on the element's HTML code and then select the "Copy XPath" option.

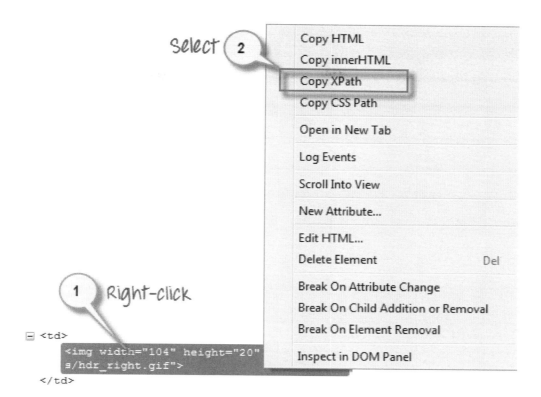

Step 3. In Selenium IDE, type one forward slash "/" in the Target box then paste the XPath that we copied in the previous step. **The entry in your Target box should now begin with two forward slashes "//".**

Step 4. Click on the Find button. Selenium IDE should be able to highlight the orange box as shown below.

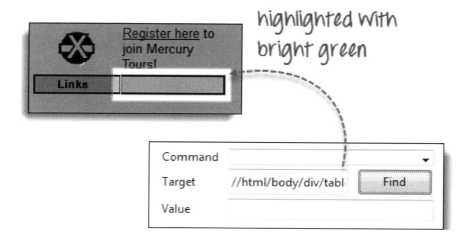

Summary

Syntax for Locator Usage

Method	Target Syntax	Example
By ID	id= *id_of_the_element*	id=email
By Name	name=*name_of_the_element*	name=username
By Name Using Filters	name=*name_of_the_elementfilter=value_of_filter*	name=tripType value=oneway
By Link Text	link=*link_text*	link=REGISTER
Tag and ID	css=*tag#id*	css=input#email
Tag and Class	css=*tag.class*	css=input.inputtext
Tag and Attribute	css=*tag[attribute=value]*	css=input[name=lastName]
Tag, Class, and Attribute	css=*tag.class[attribute=value]*	css=input.inputtext[tabindex=1]

Chapter 6: How to enhance a script using Selenium IDE

In this tutorial, we look at commands that will make your automation script more intelligent and complete.

Verify Presence of an Element

We can use following two commands to verify the presence of an element:

- **verifyElementPresent** - returns TRUE if the specified element was FOUND in the page; FALSE if otherwise

- **verifyElementNotPresent** - returns TRUE if the specified element was NOT FOUND anywhere in the page; FALSE if it is present.

The test script below verifies that the UserName text box is present within the Mercury Tours homepage while the First Name text box is not. The First Name text box is actually an element present in the Registration page of Mercury Tours, not in the homepage. strong>Verify Presence of a Certain Text

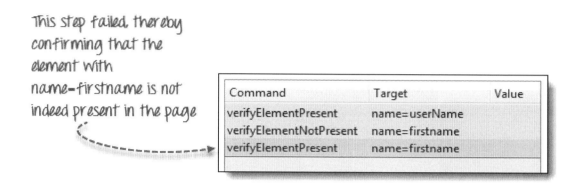

This step failed, thereby confirming that the element with name=firstname is not indeed present in the page

Command	Target	Value
verifyElementPresent	name=userName	
verifyElementNotPresent	name=firstname	
verifyElementPresent	name=firstname	

Verify Presence of a Certain Text

- **verifyTextPresent** - returns TRUE if the specified text string was FOUND somewhere in the page; FALSE if otherwise

- **verifyTextNotPresent** - returns TRUE if the specified text string was NOT FOUND anywhere in the page; FALSE if it was found

Remember that these commands are case-sensitive.

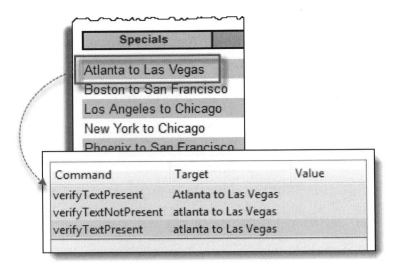

In the scenario above, "Atlanta to Las Vegas" was treated differently from "Atlanta to Las Vegas" because the letter "A" of "Atlanta" was in uppercase on the first one while lowercase on the other. When the verifyTextPresent command was used on each of them, one passed while the other failed.

Verify Specific Position of an Element

Selenium IDE indicates the position of an element by measuring (in pixels) how far it is from the left or top edge of the browser window.

- **verifyElementPositionLeft** - verifies if the specified number of pixels match the distance of the element from the left edge of the page. This will return FALSE if the value specified does not match the distance from the left edge.

- **verifyElementPositionTop** - verifies if the specified number of pixels match the distance of the element from the top edge of the page. This will return FALSE if the value specified does not match the distance from the top edge.

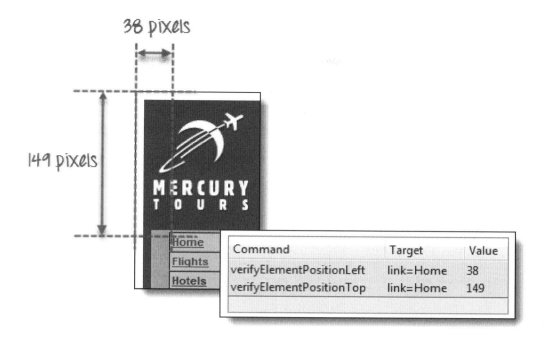

Wait commands

andWait commands

These are commands that will wait for a new page to load before moving onto the next command.

Examples are

- clickAndWait

- typeAndWait

- selectAndWait

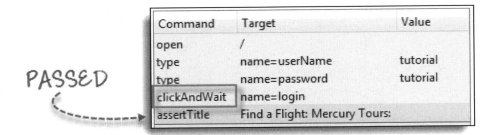

PASSED

This PASSED because "clickAndWait" was used. Selenium IDE first waited for a new page to load before executing the "assertTitle" command.

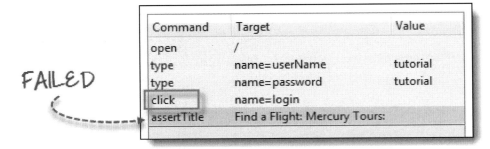

FAILED

This 2nd test case FAILED because "click" was used. Selenium IDE executed the "assertTitle" command without waiting for a new page to load.

waitFor commands

These are commands that wait for a specified condition to become true before proceeding to the next command (irrespective of loading of a new page). These commands are more appropriate to be used on AJAX-based dynamic websites that change values and elements without reloading the whole page. Examples include:

- waitForTitle

- waitForTextPresent

- waitForAlert

Consider the Facebook scenario below.

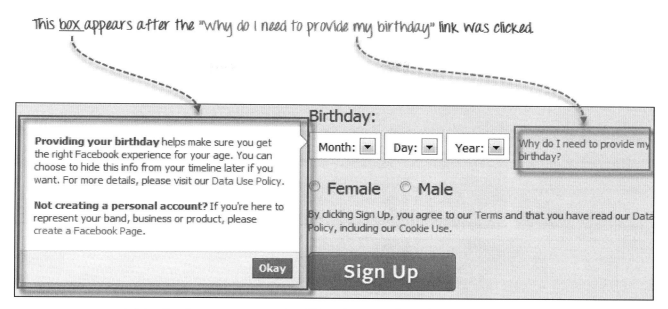

This box appears after the "why do I need to provide my birthday" link was clicked.

Birthday:

Month: ▾ Day: ▾ Year: ▾

Why do I need to provide my birthday?

Providing your birthday helps make sure you get the right Facebook experience for your age. You can choose to hide this info from your timeline later if you want. For more details, please visit our Data Use Policy.

Not creating a personal account? If you're here to represent your band, business or product, please create a Facebook Page.

Okay

○ Female ○ Male

By clicking Sign Up, you agree to our Terms and that you have read our Data Policy, including our Cookie Use.

Sign Up

Note: The box appeared without reloading the page.

We can use a combination of "click" and "waitForTextPresent" to verify the presence of the text "Providing your birthday."

Command	Target	Value
open		
click	link=Why do I need to provide my birthday?	
waitForTextPresent	Providing your birthday	
verifyTextPresent	Providing your birthday	

PASSED

We cannot use clickAndWait because no page was loaded upon clicking on the "Why do I need to provide my birthday?" link. If we do, the test will fail

Since clickAndWait was used even though no page was loaded, Selenium IDE basically waited for nothing

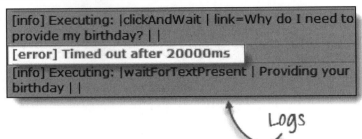

Logs

Summary

- The three most commonly used commands in verifying page elements are:
    - verifyElementPresent/ verifyElementNotPresent
    - verifyTextPresent/ verifyTextNotPresent
    - verifyElementPositionLeft/ verifyElementPositionTop
- Wait commands are classified into two:
    - andWait commands - used when a page is expected to be loaded
    - waitFor commands - used when no new page is expected to be loaded

Chapter 7: Introduction to WebDriver & Comparison with Selenium RC

Now that you have learned to create simple tests in Selenium IDE, we shall now create more powerful scripts using an advanced tool called **WebDriver**.

What is WebDriver?

WebDriver is a web automation framework that allows you to **execute your tests against different browsers**, not just Firefox (unlike Selenium IDE).

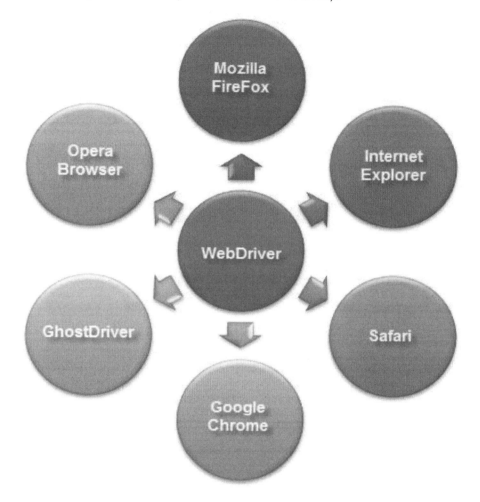

WebDriver also enables you to **use a programming language** in creating your test scripts (not possible in Selenium IDE).

- You can now use **conditional operations** like if-then-else or switch-case
- You can also perform **looping** like do-while.

Following programming languages are supported by WebDriver

- **Java**
- .Net
- **PHP**
- **Python**
- **Perl**

- Ruby

You do not have to know all of them. You just need to be knowledgeable in one. However, in this tutorial, we will be using Java with Eclipse as our IDE.

Difference between Selenium RC and Webdriver

Before the advent of WebDriver in 2006, there was another, **automation tool called Selenium Remote Control.** Both WebDriver and Selenium RC have following features:

- They both allow you to **use a programming language** in designing your test scripts.

- They both allow you to **run your tests against different browsers.**

So how do they differ? Let us discuss the answers.

1. Architecture

WebDriver's architecture is simpler than Selenium RC's.

- It controls the browser from the OS level

- All you need are your programming language's IDE (which contains your Selenium commands) and a browser.

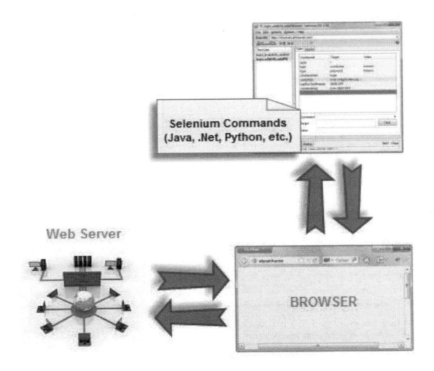

Selenium RC's architecture is way more complicated.

- You first need to launch **a separate application called Selenium Remote Control (RC) Server** before you can start testing

- The Selenium RC Server **acts as a "middleman" between your Selenium commands and your browser**

- When you begin testing, Selenium RC Server "injects" a **Javascript program called Selenium Core** into the browser.

- Once injected, Selenium Core will start receiving instructions relayed by the RC Server from your test program.

- When the instructions are received, **Selenium Core will execute them as Javascript commands.**

- The browser will obey the instructions of Selenium Core and will relay its response to the RC Server.

- The RC Server will receive the response of the browser and then display the results to you.

- RC Server will fetch the next instruction from your test script to repeat the whole cycle.

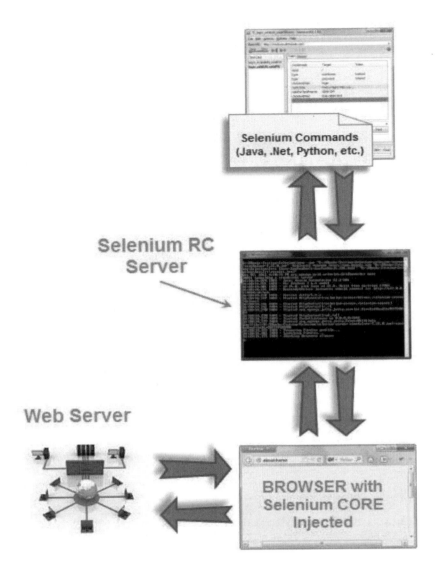

Selenium Commands
(Java, .Net, Python, etc.)

Selenium RC
Server

Web Server

BROWSER with
Selenium CORE
Injected

2. Speed

WebDriver is faster than Selenium RC since it speaks directly to the browser uses the browser's own engine to control it.

Selenium RC is slower since it uses a Javascript program called Selenium Core. This Selenium Core is the one that directly controls the browser, not you.

3. Real-life Interaction

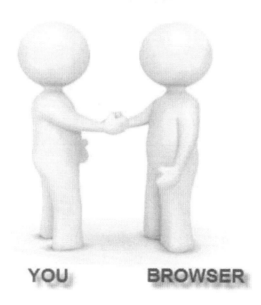

This is what happens in WebDriver

YOU   BROWSER

WebDriver interacts with page elements in a more realistic way. For example, if you have a disabled text box on a page you were testing, WebDriver really cannot enter any value in it just as how a real person cannot.

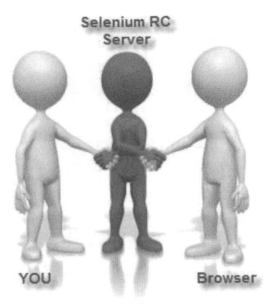

This is what happens in
Selenium RC

Selenium Core, just like other **JavaScript** codes, can access disabled elements. In the past, Selenium testers complain that Selenium Core was able to enter values to a disabled text box in their tests. Differences in API

4. API

Selenium RC's API is more matured but contains redundancies and often confusing commands. For example, most of the time, testers are confused whether to use type or typeKeys; or whether to use click, mouseDown, or mouseDownAt. Worse, **different browsers interpret each of these commands in different ways too!**

WebDriver's API is simpler than Selenium RC's. It does not contain redundant and confusing commands.

5. Browser Support

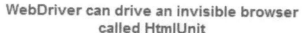

WebDriver can support the headless HtmlUnit browser

HtmlUnit is termed as "headless" because it is an invisible browser - it is GUI-less.

It is a very fast browser because no time is spent in waiting for page elements to load. This accelerates your test execution cycles.

Since it is invisible to the user, it can only be controlled through automated means.

Selenium RC cannot support the headless HtmlUnit browser. It needs a real, visible browser to operate on.

Limitations of WebDriver

WebDriver Cannot Readily Support New Browsers

Remember that WebDriver operates on the OS level. Also, remember that different browsers communicate with the OS in different ways. If a new browser comes out, it may have a different process of communicating with the OS as compared to other browsers. So, **you have to give the WebDriver team quite some time to figure that new process out** before they can implement it on the next WebDriver release.

However, it is up to the WebDriver's team of developers to decide if they should support the new browser or not.

Selenium RC Has Built-In Test Result Generator

Selenium RC automatically generates an HTML file of test results. The format of the report was pre-set by RC itself. Take a look at an example of this report below.

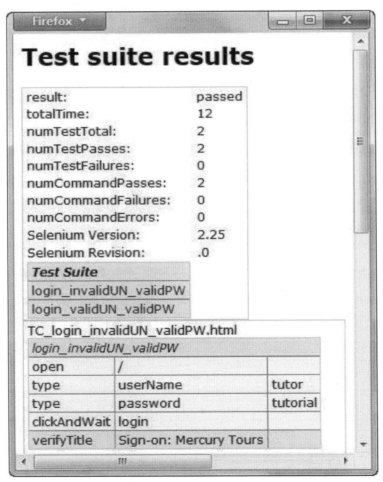

WebDriver has no built-in command that automatically generates a Test Results File. You would have to rely on your IDE's output window, or design the report yourself using the capabilities of your programming language and store it as text, HTML, etc.

Summary

- WebDriver is a tool for testing web applications **across different browsers** using different programming languages.

- You are now able to make powerful tests because WebDriver **allows you to use a programming language** of your choice in designing your tests.

- WebDriver is **faster than Selenium RC** because of its simpler architecture.

- WebDriver **directly talks to the browser** while Selenium RC needs the help of the RC Server in order to do so.

- WebDriver's API is more **concise** than Selenium RC's.

- WebDriver **can support HtmlUnit** while Selenium RC cannot.

- The only drawbacks of WebDriver are:

    - It **cannot readily support new browsers**, but Selenium RC can.

    - It **does not have a built-in command** for automatic generation of test results.

Chapter 8: Guide to install Selenium WebDriver

In this tutorial, we will install Webdriver (Java only) and Configure Eclipse

Step 1 - Install Java on your computer

Download and install the **Java Software Development Kit (JDK)**

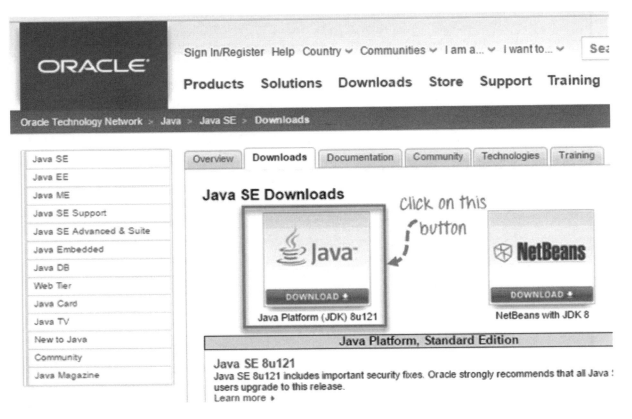

Next –

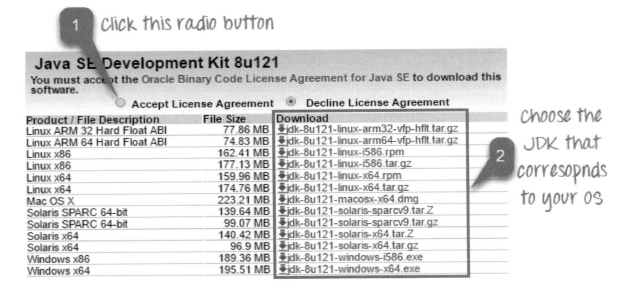

This JDK version comes bundled with Java Runtime Environment (JRE), so you do not need to download and install the JRE separately.

Step 2 - Install Eclipse IDE

Download **"Eclipse IDE for Java Developers" here**. Be sure to choose correctly between Windows 32 Bit and 64 Bit versions.

You should be able to download an exe file named "eclipse-inst-win64"

Double-click on file to Install the Eclipse. A new window will open. Click Eclipse IDE for Java Developers.

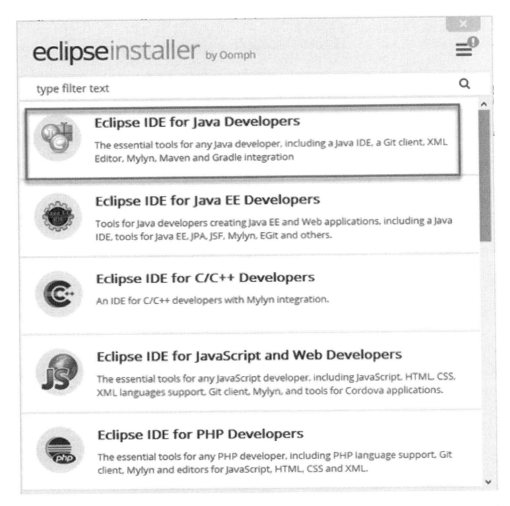

After that, a new window will open which click button marked 1 and change path to "C:\eclipse". Post that Click on Install button marked 2

After successful completion of the installation procedure, a window will appear. On that window click on Launch

This will start eclipse neon IDE for you.

Step 3 - Download the Selenium Java Client Driver

You can download the **Selenium Java Client Driver here**. You will find client drivers for other languages there, but only choose the one for Java.

this is the download for Java Client Driver

Language	Client Version	Release Date			
Java	3.0.1	2016-10-18	Download	Change log	Javadoc
C#	3.0.0	2016-10-13	Download	Change log	API docs
Ruby	3.0.0	2016-10-13	Download	Change log	API docs
Python	3.0.2	2016-11-29	Download	Change log	API docs
Javascript (Node)	3.0.0-beta-2	2016-08-07	Download	Change log	API docs

This download comes as a ZIP file named "selenium-2.25.0.zip". For simplicity, extract the contents of this ZIP file on your C drive so that you would have the directory "C:\selenium-2.25.0\". This directory contains all the JAR files that we would later import on Eclipse.

Step 4 - Configure Eclipse IDE with WebDriver

1. Launch the "eclipse.exe" file inside the "eclipse" folder that we extracted in step 2. If you followed step 2 correctly, the executable should be located on C:\eclipse\eclipse.exe.

2. When asked to select for a workspace, just accept the default location.

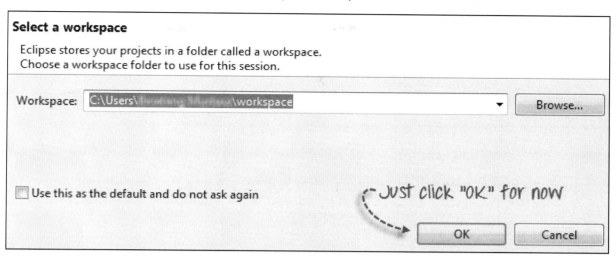

3. Create a new project through File > New > Java Project. Name the project as "newproject".

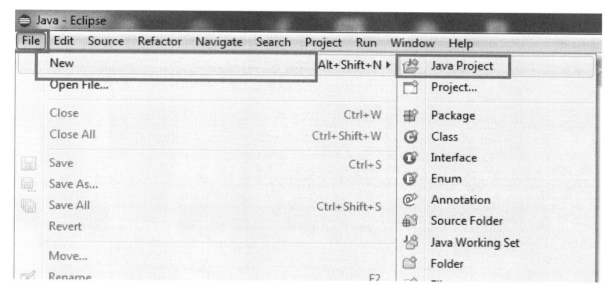

A new pop-up window will open enter details as follow

1. Project Name

2. Location to save project

3. Select an execution JRE

4. Select layout project option

5. Click on Finish button

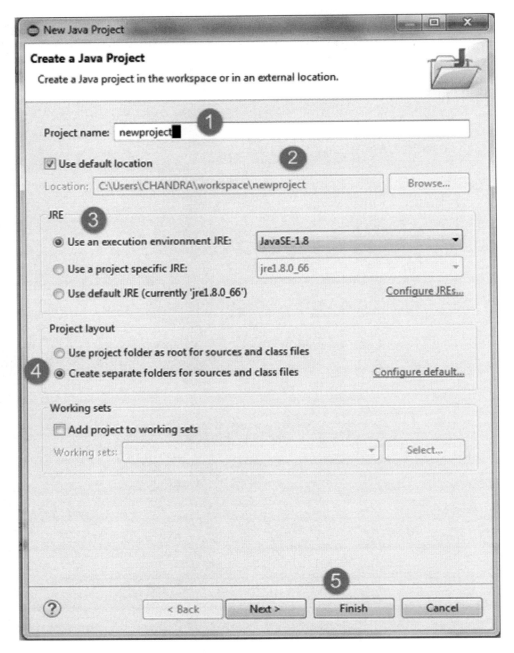

4. In this step,

1. Right-click on the newly created project and

2. Select New > Package, and name that package as "newpackage".

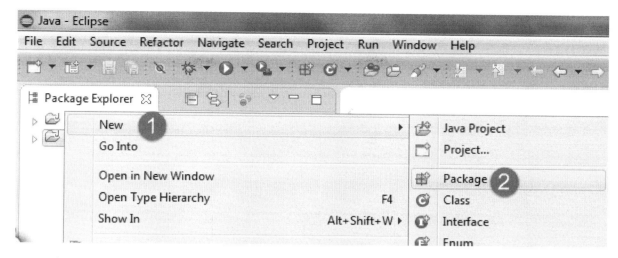

A pop-up window will open to name the package,

1. Enter the name of the package
2. Click on Finish button

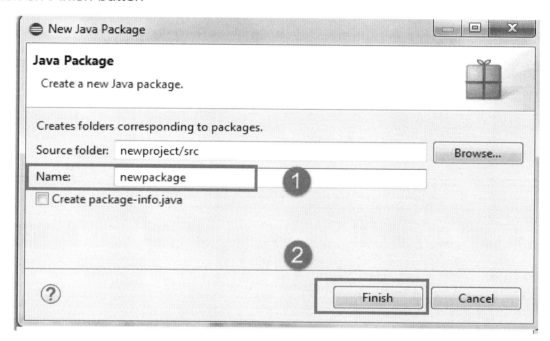

5. Create a new Java class under newpackage by right-clicking on it and then selecting-New > Class, and then name it as "MyClass". Your Eclipse IDE should look like the image below.

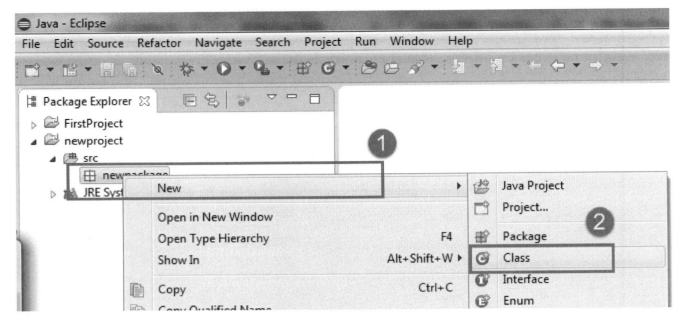

When you click on Class, a pop-up window will open, enter details as

1. Name of the class

2. Click on Finish button

This is how it looks like after creating class.

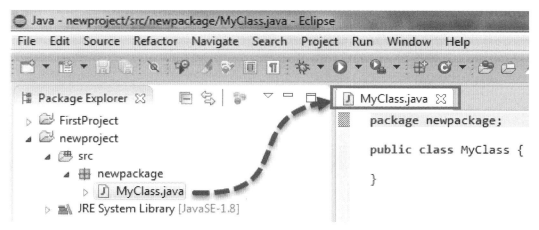

Now selenium WebDriver's into Java Build Path

In this step,

1. Right-click on "newproject" and select **Properties**.

2. On the Properties dialog, click on "Java Build Path".

3. Click on the **Libraries** tab, and then

4. Click on "Add External JARs.."

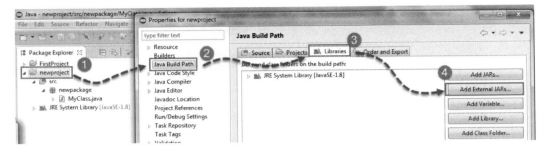

When you click on "Add External JARs.." It will open a pop-up window. Select the JAR files you want to add.

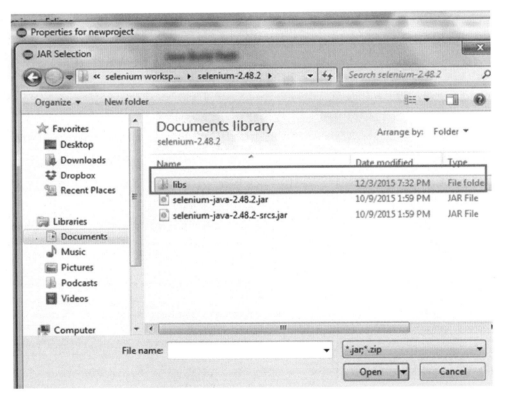

After selecting jar files, click on OK button.

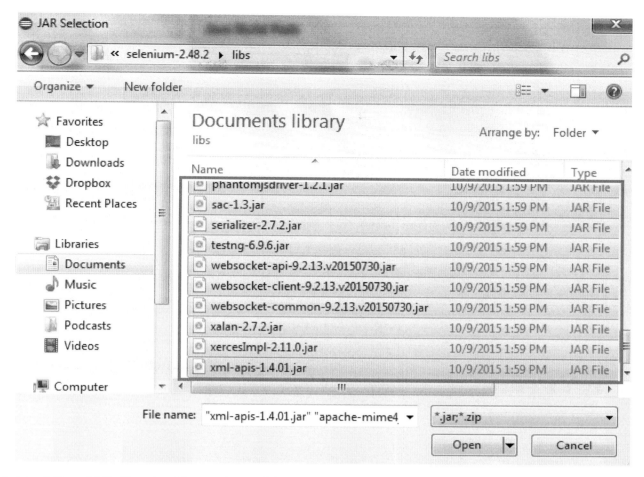

6. Add all the JAR files inside and outside the "libs" folder. Your Properties dialog should now look similar to the image below.

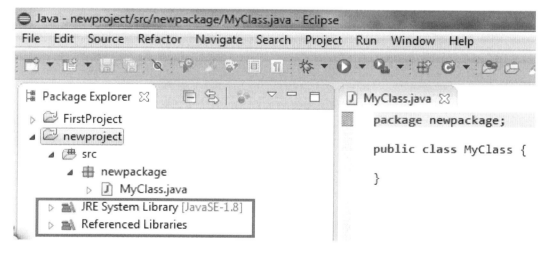

7. Finally, click OK and we are done importing Selenium libraries into our project.

Different Drivers

HTMLUnit and Firefox are two browsers that WebDriver can directly automate - meaning that no other separate component is needed to install or run while the test is being executed. For other browsers, a separate program is needed. That program is called as the **Driver Server**.

A driver server is different for each browser. For example, Internet Explorer has its own driver server which you cannot use on other browsers. Below is the list of driver servers and the corresponding browsers that use them.

You can download these drivers

Browser	Name of Driver Server	Remarks
HTMLUnit	HtmlUnitDriver	WebDriver can drive HTMLUnit using HtmlUnitDriver as driver server
Firefox	Mozilla GeckoDriver	WebDriver can drive Firefox without the need of a driver server Starting Firefox 35 & above one needs to use gecko driver created by Mozilla for automation
Internet Explorer	Internet Explorer Driver Server	Available in 32 and 64-bit versions. Use the version that corresponds to the architecture of your IE
Chrome	ChromeDriver	Though its name is just "ChromeDriver", it is, in fact, a Driver Server, not just a driver. The current version can support versions higher than Chrome v.21
Opera	OperaDriver	Though its name is just "OperaDriver", it is, in fact, a Driver Server, not just a driver.
PhantomJS	GhostDriver	PhantomJS is another headless browser just like HTMLUnit.
Safari	SafariDriver	Though its name is just "SafariDriver", it is, in fact, a Driver Server, not just a driver.

Summary

- Aside from a browser, you will need the following to start using WebDriver

- **Java Development Kit (JDK). http://www.oracle.com/technetwork/java/javase/downloads/index.html**

- **Eclipse IDE - http://www.eclipse.org/downloads/**

- **Java Client Driver - http://seleniumhq.org/download/**

- When starting a WebDriver project in Eclipse, do not forget to import the Java Client Driver files onto your project. These files will constitute your Selenium Library.

- HTMLUnit and Firefox are the only browsers that you can automate without the use of a Driver Server.

- Each other browser has its own driver server.

Chapter 9: Creating your First Script in Webdriver

Using the **Java** class "myclass" that we created in the previous tutorial, let us try to create a WebDriver script that would:

1. fetch Mercury Tours' homepage

2. verify its title

3. print out the result of the comparison

4. close it before ending the entire program.

WebDriver Code

Below is the actual WebDriver code for the logic presented by the scenario above

Note: Starting Firefox 35, you need to use gecko driver created by Mozilla for Web Driver. Also, if the code does not work, downgrade to Firefox version 47 or below. Gecko has compatibility issues with recent versions of Firefox.

```
package newproject;
import org.openqa.selenium.WebDriver;
import org.openqa.selenium.firefox.FirefoxDriver;
public class PG1 {
```

```java
public static void main(String[] args) {
    // declaration and instantiation of objects/variables
    WebDriver driver ;
    System.setProperty("webdriver.firefox.marionette","C:\\geckodriver.exe");
    driver = new FirefoxDriver();
    String baseUrl = "http://newtours.demoaut.com";
    String expectedTitle = "Welcome: Mercury Tours";
    String actualTitle = "";

    // launch Fire fox and direct it to the Base URL
    driver.get(baseUrl);

    // get the actual value of the title
    actualTitle = driver.getTitle();

    /*
     * compare the actual title of the page with the expected one and print
     * the result as "Passed" or "Failed"
     */
    if (actualTitle.contentEquals(expectedTitle)){
        System.out.println("Test Passed!");
    } else {
        System.out.println("Test Failed");
    }

    //close Fire fox
    driver.close();

    // exit the program explicitly
    System.exit(0);
    }
}
```

Explaining the code

Importing Packages

To get started, you need to import following two packages:

1. **org.openqa.selenium.***- contains the WebDriver class needed to instantiate a new browser loaded with a specific driver

2. **org.openqa.selenium.firefox.FirefoxDriver** - contains the FirefoxDriver class needed to instantiate a Firefox-specific driver onto the browser instantiated by the WebDriver class

If your test needs more complicated actions such as accessing another class, taking browser screenshots, or manipulating external files, definitely you will need to import more packages.

Instantiating objects and variables

Normally, this is how a driver object is instantiated.

```
WebDriver driver = new FirefoxDriver();
```

A FirefoxDriver class with no parameters means that the default Firefox profile will be launched by our Java program. The default Firefox profile is similar to launching Firefox in safe mode (no extensions are loaded).

For convenience, we saved the Base URL and the expected title as variables.

Launching a Browser Session

WebDriver's **get()** method is used to launch a new browser session and directs it to the URL that you specify as its parameter.

```
driver.get(baseUrl);
```

Get the Actual Page Title

The WebDriver class has the **getTitle()** method that is always used to obtain the page title of the currently loaded page.

```
actualTitle = driver.getTitle();
```

Compare the Expected and Actual Values

This portion of the code simply uses a basic Java if-else structure to compare the actual title with the expected one.

```
if (actualTitle.contentEquals(expectedTitle)) {
    System.out.println("Test Passed!");
} else {
    System.out.println("Test Failed!");
}
```

Terminating a Browser Session

The "**close()**" method is used to close the browser window.

```
driver.close();
```

Terminating the Entire Program

If you use this command without closing all browser windows first, your whole Java program will end while leaving the browser window open.

```
System.exit(0);
```

Running the Test

There are two ways to execute code in Eclipse IDE.

1. On Eclipse's menu bar, click **Run > Run.**

2. Press **Ctrl+F11** to run the entire code.

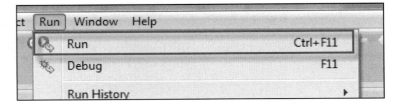

If you did everything correctly, Eclipse would output "Test Passed!"

Locating GUI Elements

Locating elements in WebDriver is done by using the "**findElement(By.LOCATOR())**" method. The "locator" part of the code is same as any of the locators previously discussed in the Selenium IDE chapters of these tutorials. Infact, it is recommended that you locate GUI elements using IDE and once successfully identified export the code to webdriver.

Here is a sample code that locates an element by its id. Facebook is used as the Base URL.

```java
package newproject;
import org.openqa.selenium.By;
import org.openqa.selenium.WebDriver;
import org.openqa.selenium.firefox.FirefoxDriver;

public class PG2 {
    public static void main(String[] args) {
        System.setProperty("webdriver.firefox.marionette","C:\\geckodriver.exe");
        WebDriver driver = new FirefoxDriver();
        String baseUrl = "http://www.facebook.com";
        String tagName = "";

        driver.get(baseUrl);
        tagName = driver.findElement(By.id("email")).getTagName();
        System.out.println(tagName);
        driver.close();
        System.exit(0);
    }
}
```

We used the **getTagName()** method to extract the tag name of that particular element whose id is "email". When run, this code should be able to correctly identify the tag name "input" and will print it out on Eclipse's Console window.

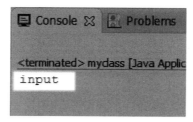

Summary for locating elements

Variation	Description	Sample
By.**className**	finds elements based on the value of	FindElement(By.className("someClassName"))

	the "class" attribute	
By.**cssSelector**	finds elements based on the driver's underlying CSS Selector engine	findElement(By.cssSelector("input#email"))
By.**id**	locates elements by the value of their "id" attribute	findElement(By.id("someId"))
By.**linkText**	finds a link element by the exact text it displays	findElement(By.linkText("REGISTRATION"))
By.**name**	locates elements by the value of the "name" attribute	findElement(By.name("someName"))
By.**partialLinkText**	locates elements that contain the given link text	findElement(By.partialLinkText("REG"))
By.**tagName**	locates elements by their tag name	findElement(By.tagName("div"))
By.**xpath**	locates elements via XPath	findElement(By.xpath ("//ht ml/body/div/table/tbody/tr/td[2]/table/tbody/tr[4]/td/table/tb ody/tr/td[2]/table/tbody/tr[2]/td[3]/ form/table/tbody/tr[5]"))

Note on Using findElement(By.cssSelector())

By.cssSelector() does not support the "contains" feature. Consider the Selenium IDE code below -

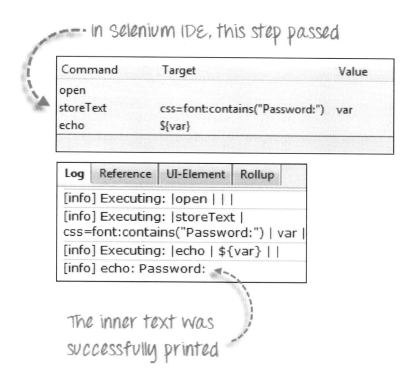

In Selenium IDE above, the entire test passed. However in the WebDriver script below, the same test generated an error because WebDriver does not support the "contains" keyword when used in the By.cssSelector() method.

```
 1  package mypackage;
 2
 3⊖ import org.openqa.selenium.*;
 4  import org.openqa.selenium.firefox.FirefoxDriver;
 5
 6  public class myclass {
 7
 8⊖     public static void main(String[] args) {
 9          WebDriver driver = new FirefoxDriver();
10          String baseUrl = "http://newtours.demoaut.com";
11          String var = "";
12
13          driver.get(baseUrl);
14          var = driver.findElement(By.cssSelector("font:contains('Password:')")).getText();
15          System.out.println(var);
16
17          driver.close();
18          System.exit(0);
19      }
20  }
21
```

this line caused an error because the 'contains' keyword is not supported by By.cssselector() in WebDriver ---→

```
        at mypackage.myclass.main(myclass.java:14)
Caused by: org.openqa.selenium.remote.ErrorHandler$UnknownServerException: An invalid or illegal string was specified
```

Eclipse IDE reports that error was caused by line 14, the line where By.cssselector() was used ----→

Common Commands

Instantiating Web Elements

Instead of using the long "driver.findElement(By.locator())" syntax every time you will access a particular element, we can instantiate a WebElement object for it. The WebElement class is contained in the "org.openqa.selenium.*" package.

```
WebElement myElement = driver.findElement(By.id("username"));
myElement.sendKeys("tutorial");
```

Clicking on an Element

Clicking is perhaps the most common way of interacting with web elements. **The click() method is used to simulate the clicking of any element.** The following example shows how click() was used to click on Mercury Tours' "Sign-In" button.

```
driver.findElement(By.name("login")).click();
```

Following things must be noted when using the click() method.

- **It does not take any parameter/argument.**

- The method **automatically waits for a new page to load** if applicable.

- The element to be clicked-on, **must be visible** (height and width must not be equal to zero).

Get Commands

Get commands fetch various important information about the page/element. Here are some important "get" commands you must be familiar with.

get() SAMPLE USAGE:	• It automatically opens a new browser window and fetches the page that you specify inside its parentheses. • It is the counterpart of Selenium IDE's "open" command. • The parameter must be a **String** object.
getTitle() SAMPLE USAGE:	• Needs no parameters • Fetches the title of the current page • Leading and trailing white spaces are trimmed • Returns a null string if the page has no title
getPageSource() SAMPLE USAGE:	• Needs no parameters • Returns the **source code of the page** as a String value
getCurrentUrl() SAMPLE USAGE:	• Needs no parameters • Fetches the string representing the **current URL** that the browser is looking at
getText() SAMPLE USAGE:	• Fetches the **inner text** of the element that you specify

Navigate commands

These commands allow you to refresh, go-into and switch back and forth between different web pages.

navigate().to() SAMPLE USAGE:	• It automatically **opens a new browser window and fetches the page** that you specify inside its parentheses. • **It does exactly the same thing as the get() method.**
navigate().refresh() SAMPLE USAGE:	• Needs no parameters. • It **refreshes** the current page.
navigate().back() SAMPLE USAGE:	• Needs no parameters • Takes you **back by one page** on the browser's history.
navigate().forward() SAMPLE USAGE:	• Needs no parameters • Takes you **forward by one page** on the browser's history.

Closing and Quitting Browser Windows

close() SAMPLE USAGE:	• Needs no parameters • **It closes only the browser window that WebDriver is currently controlling.**
quit() SAMPLE USAGE:	• Needs no parameters • **It closes all windows that WebDriver has opened.**

close()
- will only close a
single window

quit()
- will close all
windows

To clearly illustrate the difference between close() and quit(), try to execute the code below. It uses a webpage that automatically pops up a window upon page load and opens up another after exiting.

using close()

```
public static void main(String[] args) {
    WebDriver driver = new FirefoxDriver();
    driver.get("http://www.popuptest.com/popuptest2.html");
    driver.close();
}
```

Notice that only the parent browser window was closed and not the two pop-up windows.

After executing driver.close(), these two pop-ups remained. only the parent window was closed.

But if you use quit(), all windows will be closed - not just the parent one. Try running the code below and you will notice that the two pop-ups above will automatically be closed as well.

```
package newproject;
import org.openqa.selenium.WebDriver;
import org.openqa.selenium.firefox.FirefoxDriver;


public class PG3 {
    public static void main(String[] args) {
        System.setProperty("webdriver.firefox.marionette","C:\\geckodriver.exe");
        WebDriver driver = new FirefoxDriver();
        driver.get("http://www.popuptest.com/popuptest2.html");
        driver.quit();  // using QUIT all windows will close
    }
}
```

Switching Between Frames

To access GUI elements in a Frame, we should first direct WebDriver to focus on the frame or pop-up window first before we can access elements within them. Let us take, for example, the web page **http://demo.guru99.com/selenium/deprecated.html**

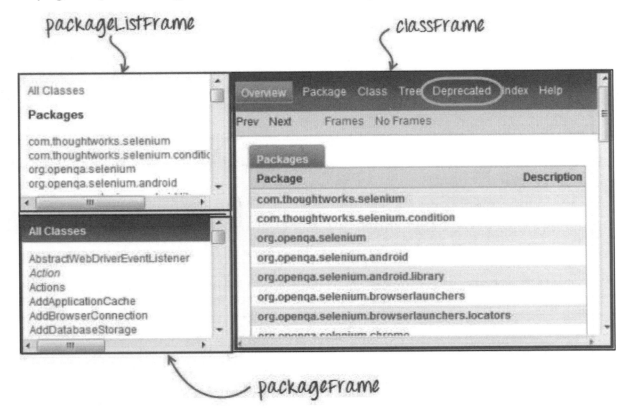

This page has 3 frames whose "name" attributes are indicated above. We wish to access the "Deprecated" link encircled above in yellow. In order to do that, we must first instruct

WebDriver to switch to the "classFrame" frame using the **"switchTo().frame()"** method. We will use the name attribute of the frame as the parameter for the "frame()" part.

```
package newproject;
import org.openqa.selenium.By;
import org.openqa.selenium.WebDriver;
import org.openqa.selenium.firefox.FirefoxDriver;
public class PG4 {
        public static void main(String[] args) {

        System.setProperty("webdriver.firefox.marionette","C:\\geckodriver.exe");
                    WebDriver driver = new FirefoxDriver();
            driver.get("http://demo.guru99.com/selenium/deprecated.html");
            driver.switchTo().frame("classFrame");
            driver.findElement(By.linkText("Deprecated")).click();
            driver.close();
        }
}
```

After executing this code, you will see that the "classFrame" frame is taken to the "Deprecated API" page, meaning that our code was successfully able to access the "Deprecated" link.

Switching Between Pop-up Windows

WebDriver allows pop-up windows like alerts to be displayed, unlike in Selenium IDE. To access the elements within the alert (such as the message it contains), we must use the **"switchTo().alert()"** method. In the code below, we will use this method to access the alert box and then retrieve its message using the **"getText()"** method, and then automatically close the alert box using the **"switchTo().alert().accept()"** method.

First, head over to **http://jsbin.com/usidix/1** and manually click the "Go!" button there and see for yourself the message text.

Lets see the WebDriver code to do this-

```
package mypackage;

import org.openqa.selenium.By;
import org.openqa.selenium.WebDriver;
import org.openqa.selenium.firefox.FirefoxDriver;

public class myclass {

    public static void main(String[] args) {
        System.setProperty("webdriver.firefox.marionette","C:\\geckodriver.exe");
        WebDriver driver = new FirefoxDriver();
        String alertMessage = "";

        driver.get("http://jsbin.com/usidix/1");
        driver.findElement(By.cssSelector("input[value=\"Go!\"]")).click();
        alertMessage = driver.switchTo().alert().getText();
        driver.switchTo().alert().accept();

        System.out.println(alertMessage);
        driver.quit();

    }
}
```

On the Eclipse console, notice that the printed alert message is:

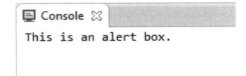

Waits

There are two kinds of waits.

1. Implicit wait - used to set the default waiting time throughout the program
2. Explicit wait - used to set the waiting time for a particular instance only

Implicit Wait

- It is simpler to code than Explicit Waits.
- It is usually declared in the instantiation part of the code.

- You will only need one additional package to import.

To start using an implicit wait, you would have to import this package into your code.

```
import java.util.concurrent.TimeUnit;
```

Then on the instantiation part of your code, add this.

```
driver.manage().timeouts().implicitlyWait(10, TimeUnit.SECONDS);
```

this means that you are setting 10 seconds as your default wait time. You can change "10" and "SECONDS" to any number and time unit you want.

Explicit Wait

Explicit waits are done using the WebDriverWait and ExpectedCondition classes. For the following example, we shall wait up to 10 seconds for an element whose id is "username" to become visible before proceeding to the next command. Here are the steps.

Step 1

Import these two packages:

```
import org.openqa.selenium.support.ui.ExpectedConditions;
import org.openqa.selenium.support.ui.WebDriverWait;
```

Step 2

Declare a WebDriverWait variable. In this example, we will use "myWaitVar" as the name of the variable.

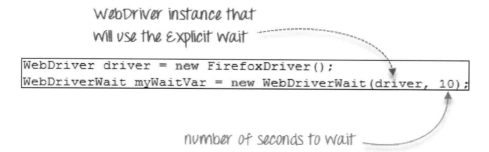

WebDriver instance that will use the Explicit wait

```
WebDriver driver = new FirefoxDriver();
WebDriverWait myWaitVar = new WebDriverWait(driver, 10);
```

number of seconds to wait

Step 3

Use myWaitVar with ExpectedConditions on portions where you need the explicit wait to occur. In this case, we will use explicit wait on the "username" (Mercury Tours HomePage) input before we type the text "tutorial" onto it.

```
myWaitVar.until(ExpectedConditions.visibilityOfElementLocated(By.id("username")));
driver.findElement(By.id("username")).sendKeys("tutorial");
```

Conditions

Following methods are used in conditional and looping operations --

- **isEnabled()** is used when you want to verify whether a certain element is enabled or not before executing a command.

for convenience, we saved the element with id="username" as an instance of the WebElement class. The WebElement class is contained in the package `org.openqa.selenium.*`

```
WebElement txtbox_username = driver.findElement(By.id("username"));
if(txtbox_username.isEnabled()){
    txtbox_username.sendKeys("tutorial");
}
```

- **isDisplayed()** is used when you want to verify whether a certain element is displayed or not before executing a command.

```
do{
    //do something here
}while (driver.findElement(By.id("username")).isDisplayed());
```

- **isSelected()** is used when you want to verify whether a certain **check box, radio button, or option in a drop-down box** is selected. It does not work on other elements.

```
//"one-way" and "two-way" are radio buttons
if (driver.findElement(By.id("one-way")).isSelected()) {
    driver.findElement(By.id("two-way")).click();
}
```

Using ExpectedConditions

The ExpectedConditions class offers a wider set of conditions that you can use in conjunction with WebDriverWait's until() method.

Below are some of the most common ExpectedConditions methods.

- **alertIsPresent()** - waits until an alert box is displayed.

```
if (myWaitVar.until(ExpectedConditions.alertIsPresent()) != null) {
    System.out.println("alert is present!");
}
```

- **elementToBeClickable()** - Waits until an element is visible and, at the same time, enabled. The sample code below will wait until the element with id="username" to become visible and enabled first before assigning that element as a WebElement variable named "txtUserName".

```
WebElement txtUserName = myWaitVar.until(ExpectedConditions
        .elementToBeClickable(By.id("username")));
```

- **frameToBeAvailableAndSwitchToIt()** - Waits until the given frame is already available, and then automatically switches to it.

> This will automatically switch to the
> "VIEWIFRAME" frame once it becomes available.

```
myWaitVar.until(ExpectedConditions
        .frameToBeAvailableAndSwitchToIt("viewIFRAME"));
```

Catching Exceptions

When using isEnabled(), isDisplayed(), and isSelected(), WebDriver assumes that the element already exists on the page. Otherwise, it will throw a **NoSuchElementException**. To avoid this, we should use a try-catch block so that the program will not be interrupted.

```
WebElement txtbox_username = driver.findElement(By.id("username"));
try{

    if(txtbox_username.isEnabled()){
        txtbox_username.sendKeys("tutorial");
    }
}


catch(NoSuchElementException nsee){
    System.out.println(nsee.toString());
}
```

If you use explicit waits, the type of exception that you should catch is the "TimeoutException".

```
WebDriverWait myWaitVar = new WebDriverWait(driver, 3);
try {
    myWaitVar.until(ExpectedConditions.visibilityOfElementLocated(By
            .id("username")));
    driver.findElement(By.id("username")).sendKeys("tutorial");
} catch (TimeoutException toe) {
    System.out.println(toe.toString());
}
```

Summary

- To start using the WebDriver API, you must import at least these two packages.
    - **org.openqa.selenium.***
    - **org.openqa.selenium.firefox.FirefoxDriver**
- The **get()** method is the equivalent of Selenium IDE's "open" command.
- Locating elements in WebDriver is done by using the **findElementBy()** method.
- The following are the available options for locating elements in WebDriver:
    - By.**className**
    - By.**cssSelector**
    - By.**id**
    - By.**linkText**
    - By.**name**
    - By.**partialLinkText**
    - By.**tagName**
    - By.**xpath**
- TheBy.cssSelector() **does not** support the **"contains"** feature.
- You can instantiate an element using the **WebElement** class.
- Clicking on an element is done by using the **click()** method.
- WebDriver provides these useful **get commands**:
    - get()
    - getTitle()
    - getPageSource()

- getCurrentUrl()

- getText()

- WebDriver provides these useful **navigation commands**

  - navigate().forward()

  - navigate().back()

  - navigate().to()

  - navigate().refresh()

- The close() and quit() methods are used to close browser windows. **Close()** is used to close a single window; while **quit()** is used to close all windows associated to the parent window that the WebDriver object was controlling.

- The **switchTo().frame()** and **switchTo().alert()** methods are used to direct WebDriver's focus onto a frame or alert, respectively.

- **Implicit waits** are used to set the waiting time throughout the program, while **explicit waits** are used only on specific portions.

- You can use the **isEnabled(), isDisplayed(),isSelected(),** and a combination of **WebDriverWait** and **ExpectedConditions** methods when verifying the state of an element. However, they do not verify if the element exists.

- When isEnabled(), isDisplayed(),or isSelected() was called while the element was not existing, WebDriver will throw a **NoSuchElementException**.

- When WebDriverWait and ExpectedConditions methods were called while the element was not existing, WebDriver would throw a **TimeoutException**.

Chapter 10: Accessing Forms in Webdriver

In this tutorial, we will learn how to access forms and its elements using Webdriver

Accessing Form Elements

Input Box

Input boxes refer to either of these two types:

1. **Text Fields**- text boxes that accept typed values and show them as they are.

2. **Password Fields**- text boxes that accept typed values but mask them as a series of special characters (commonly dots and asterisks) to avoid sensitive values to be displayed.

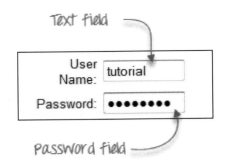

Entering Values in Input Boxes

The **sendKeys()** method is used to enter values into input boxes.

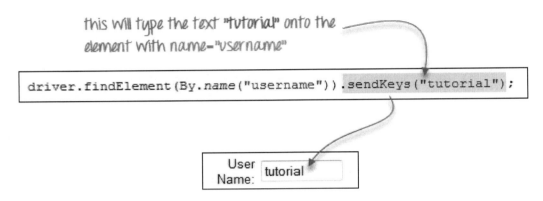

Deleting Values in Input Boxes

The **clear()** method is used to delete the text in an input box. **This method does not need any parameter**. The code snippet below will clear out the text "tutorial" in the User Name text box.

```
driver.findElement(By.name("userName")).clear();
```

Radio Button

Toggling a radio button on is done using the **click()** method.

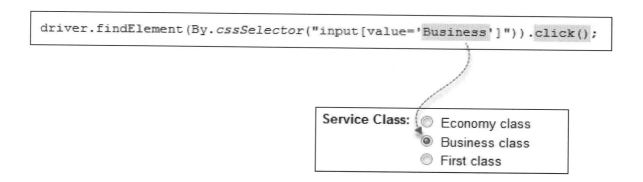

```
driver.findElement(By.cssSelector("input[value='Business']")).click();
```

Service Class: ◉ Economy class
                ◉ Business class
                ◉ First class

Check Box

Toggling a check box on/off is also done using the **click()** method.

The code below will click on Facebook's "Keep me logged in" check box twice and then output the result as TRUE when it is toggled on, and FALSE if it is toggled off.

```
public static void main(String[] args) {
    WebDriver driver = new FirefoxDriver();
    String baseURL = "http://www.facebook.com";

    driver.get(baseURL);
    WebElement chkFBPersist = driver.findElement(By.id("persist_box"));
    for(int i=0; i<2; i++){
        chkFBPersist.click();
        System.out.println(chkFBPersist.isSelected());
    }
    driver.quit();
}
```

Email or Phone

☑ Keep me logged in

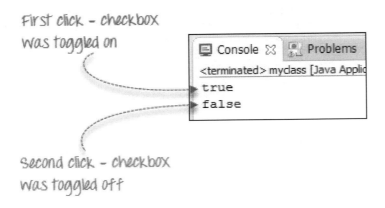

First click - checkbox was toggled on

Second click - checkbox was toggled off

Links

Links also are accessed by using the **click()** method.

Consider the below link found in Mercury Tours' homepage.

You can access this link using linkText() or partialLinkText() together with click(). Either of the two lines below will be able to access the "Register here" link shown above.

```
driver.findElement(By.linkText("Register here")).click();
```

```
driver.findElement(By.partialLinkText("here")).click();
```

Submitting a Form

The **submit()** method is used to submit a form. This is an alternative to clicking the form's submit button.

You can use submit() on any element within the form, not just on the submit button itself.

```
driver.findElement(By.name("userName")).sendKeys("tutorial");
driver.findElement(By.name("password")).sendKeys("tutorial");
driver.findElement(By.name("password")).submit();
```

*submit() was used on the password text
box instead of on the sign-in button.*

**When submit() is used, WebDriver will look up the DOM to know which form the
element belongs to, and then trigger its submit function.**

Here is the complete code

```java
package newPackage;

import org.openqa.selenium.By;
import org.openqa.selenium.WebDriver;
import org.openqa.selenium.WebElement;
import org.openqa.selenium.firefox.FirefoxDriver;
import org.openqa.selenium.support.ui.ExpectedConditions;
import org.openqa.selenium.support.ui.WebDriverWait;

public class Test {

        public static void main(String[] args) {

        // declaration and instantiation of objects/variables
        WebDriver driver ;
        System.setProperty("webdriver.firefox.marionette","C:\\geckodriver.exe");
        driver = new FirefoxDriver();

        //Create explicit wait.
        WebDriverWait myWait = new WebDriverWait(driver, 10);

        String baseUrl = "http://newtours.demoaut.com/";
        driver.get(baseUrl);

        //wait until text box load.
        myWait.until(ExpectedConditions.visibilityOfElementLocated(By.name("userName")));

        // Enter value into textbox
        driver.findElement(By.name("userName")).sendKeys ("tutorial");

        // Delete value from textbox
        driver.findElement(By.name("userName")).clear();
```

```
// Access Links
driver.findElement(By.linkText("Register here")).click();
driver.findElement(By.partialLinkText("SIGN-ON")).click();

// Enter value into textbox and SUBMIT
driver.findElement(By.name("userName")).sendKeys ("tutorial");
driver.findElement(By.name("password")).sendKeys ("tutorial");
driver.findElement(By.name("password")).submit();

// Select Radio Button
driver.findElement(By.cssSelector("input[value=Business]")).click();

//Select CheckBox
String baseURL = "http://demo.guru99.com/sele...";
driver.get(baseURL);

//Create an Explicit wait.
WebDriverWait myWait2 = new WebDriverWait(driver, 10);
myWait2.until(ExpectedConditions.visibilityOfElementLocated(By.id("persist_box")));

WebElement chkFBPersist = driver.findElement(By.id("persist_box"));
for (int i=0; i<2; i++) {
        chkFBPersist.click ();
        System.out.println(chkFBPersist.isSelected());
}

driver.quit();
System.exit(0);
}
}
```

Summary

- The table below summarizes the commands to access each type of element discussed above.

Element	Command	Description
Input Box	SENDKEYS()	used to enter values onto text boxes
	CLEAR()	used to clear text boxes of its current value
Check	CLICK()	used to toggle the element on/off

Box, Radio Button,		
Links	CLICK()	used to click on the link and wait for page load to complete before proceeding to the next command.
Submit Button	SUBMIT()	

- WebDriver allows selection of more than one option in a multiple SELECT element.

- You can use the submit() method on any element within the form. WebDriver will automatically trigger the submit function of the form where that element belongs to.

Chapter 11: Accessing Links & Tables using Selenium Webdriver

In this tutorial, we are going to learn about accessing links & Tables using Webdriver

Part 1) Accessing Links

Links Matching a Criterion

Links can be accessed using an exact or partial match of their link text. The examples below provide scenarios where multiple matches would exist and would explain how WebDriver would deal with them.

Exact Match

Accessing links using their exact link text is done through the By.linkText() method. However, if there are two links that have the very same link text, this method will only access the first one. Consider the HTML code below

```
<html>
    <head>
        <title>Sample</title>
    </head>
    <body>
        <a href="http://www.google.com">click here</a>
        <br>
        <a href="http://www.fb.com">click here</a>
    </body>
</html>
```

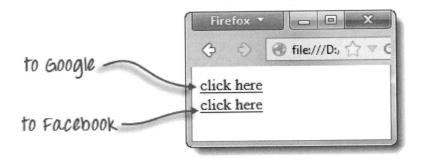

to Google

to Facebook

When you try to run the WebDriver code below, you will be accessing the first "click here" link

```java
public static void main(String[] args) {
    String baseUrl = "file:///D:/newhtml.html";
    WebDriver driver = new FirefoxDriver();

    driver.get(baseUrl);
    driver.findElement(By.LinkText("click here")).click();
    System.out.println("Title of page is: " + driver.getTitle());
    driver.quit();
}
```

As a result, you will automatically be taken to Google.

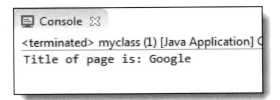

Partial Match

Accessing links using a portion of their link text is done using the **By.partialLinkText()** method. If you specify a partial link text that has multiple matches, only the first match will be accessed. Consider the HTML code below.

```
<html>
    <head>
        <title>Partial Match</title>
    </head>
    <body>
        <a href="http://www.google.com">go here</a>
        <br>
        <a href="http://www.fb.com">click here</a>
    </body>
</html>
```

When you execute the WebDriver code below, you will still be taken to Google.

```
public static void main(String[] args) {
    String baseUrl = "file:///D:/partial_match.html";
    WebDriver driver = new FirefoxDriver();

    driver.get(baseUrl);
    driver.findElement(By.partialLinkText("here")).click();
    System.out.println("Title of page is: " + driver.getTitle());
    driver.quit();
}
```

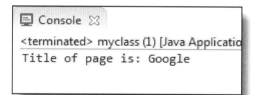

Case-sensitivity

The parameters for **By.linkText()** and **By.partialLinkText()** are both case-sensitive, meaning that capitalization matters. For example, in Mercury Tours' homepage, there are two links that contain the text "egis" - one is the "REGISTER" link found at the top menu, and the other is the "Register here" link found at the lower right portion of the page.

The link at the top menu

The link at the lower
right portion of the page

Though both links contain the character sequence "egis," the 0"By.partialLinkText()" method will access these two links separately depending on the capitalization of the characters. See the sample code below.

```java
public static void main(String[] args) {
    String baseUrl = "http://newtours.demoaut.com/";
    WebDriver driver = new FirefoxDriver();

    driver.get(baseUrl);

    String theLinkText = driver.findElement(By
            .partialLinkText("egis"))
            .getText();
    System.out.println(theLinkText);
    theLinkText = driver.findElement(By
            .partialLinkText("EGIS"))
            .getText();
    System.out.println(theLinkText);

    driver.quit();
}
```

```
Console 🔲
<terminated> myclass (1)
Register here
REGISTER
```

All Links

One of the common procedures in web **Testing** is to test if all the links present within the page are working. This can be conveniently done using a combination of the **Java for-each loop** and the **By.tagName("a")** method. The WebDriver code below checks each link from the Mercury Tours homepage to determine those that are working and those that are still under construction.

```java
package newproject;

import java.util.List;
import java.util.concurrent.TimeUnit;
import org.openqa.selenium.*;
import org.openqa.selenium.firefox.FirefoxDriver;
```

```java
public class PG5
{
        public static void main(String[] args) {

        System.setProperty("webdriver.firefox.marionette","C:\\geckodriver.exe");
                String baseUrl = "http://newtours.demoaut.com/";
                WebDriver driver = new FirefoxDriver();
                String underConsTitle = "Under Construction: Mercury Tours";
                driver.manage().timeouts().implicitlyWait(5, TimeUnit.SECONDS);

                driver.get(baseUrl);
                List<WebElement> linkElements = driver.findElements(By.tagName("a"));
                String[] linkTexts = new String[linkElements.size()];
                int i = 0;

                //extract the link texts of each link element
                for (WebElement e : linkElements) {
                    linkTexts[i] = e.getText();
                    i++;
                }

                //test each link
                for (String t : linkTexts) {
                    driver.findElement(By.linkText(t)).click();
                    if (driver.getTitle().equals(underConsTitle)) {
                        System.out.println("\"" + t + "\""
                                + " is under construction.");
                    } else {
                        System.out.println("\"" + t + "\""
                                + " is working.");
                    }
                    driver.navigate().back();
                }
                driver.quit();

        }
}
```

The output should be similar to the one indicated below.

```
Console ⨯

<terminated> myclass (1) [Java Application] C:\Program Files\Java\jre7\bin\j
"Home" is working.
"Flights" is working.
"Hotels" is under construction.
"Car Rentals" is under construction.
"Cruises" is working.
"Destinations" is under construction.
"Vacations" is under construction.
"SIGN-ON" is working.
"REGISTER" is working.
"SUPPORT" is under construction.
"CONTACT" is under construction.
"your destination" is under construction.
"featured vacation destinations" is under construction.
"Register here" is working.
"Business Travel @ About.com" is working.
"Salon Travel" is working.
```

Links Outside and Inside a Block

The latest HTML5 standard allows the <a> tags to be placed inside and outside of block-level tags like <div>, <p>, or <h1>. The "By.linkText()" and "By.partialLinkText()" methods can access a link located outside and inside these block-level elements. Consider the HTML code below.

```
<body>
    <p>
        <a href="http://www.google.com">Inside a block-level tag.</a>
    </p>

    <br>
    <a href="http://www.fb.com">
        <div>
            <span>Outside a block-level tag.</span>
        </div>
    </a>
</body>
```

The WebDriver code below accesses both of these links using By.partialLinkText() method.

```
public static void main(String[] args) {
    String baseUrl = "file:///D:/Links%20Outside%20and%20Inside%20a%20Block.html";
    WebDriver driver = new FirefoxDriver();

    driver.get(baseUrl);
    driver.findElement(By.partialLinkText("Inside")).click();
    System.out.println(driver.getTitle());
    driver.navigate().back();
    driver.findElement(By.partialLinkText("Outside")).click();
    System.out.println(driver.getTitle());
    driver.quit();
}
```

```
Console ⌗
<terminated> myclass (1) [Java Application] C:\Program Files\Java\jre7
Google
Welcome to Facebook - Log In, Sign Up or Learn More
```

The output above confirms that both links were accessed successfully because their respective page titles were retrieved correctly.

Accessing Image Links

Image links are images that act as references to other sites or sections within the same page. Since they are images, we cannot use the By.linkText() and By.partialLinkText() methods because image links basically have no link texts at all. In this case, we should resort to using either By.cssSelector or By.xpath. The first method is more preferred because of its simplicity.

In the example below, we will access the "Facebook" logo on the upper left portion of Facebook's Password Recovery page.

this is the image link that we will access

```
<a class="lfloat" title="Go to Facebook Home" href="/">
    <i class="fb_logo img sp_6jxgq1 sx_df432d">
        <u>Facebook logo</u>
    </i>
</a>
```

We will use By.cssSelector and the element's "title" attribute to access the image link. And then we will verify if we are taken to Facebook's homepage.

```java
package newproject;

import org.openqa.selenium.*;
//import org.openqa.selenium.WebDriver;
import org.openqa.selenium.firefox.FirefoxDriver;

public class PG6 {

    public static void main(String[] args) {
    String baseUrl = "https://www.facebook.com/login/identify?ctx=recover";
    System.setProperty("webdriver.firefox.marionette","C:\\geckodriver.exe");
    WebDriver driver = new FirefoxDriver();

    driver.get(baseUrl);
    //click on the "Facebook" logo on the upper left portion
    driver.findElement(By.cssSelector("a[title=\"Go to Facebook home\"]")).click();

    //verify that we are now back on Facebook's homepage
    if (driver.getTitle().equals("Facebook - Log In or Sign Up")) {
```

```
        System.out.println("We are back at Facebook's homepage");
    } else {
        System.out.println("We are NOT in Facebook's homepage");
    }
    driver.close();
    }
}
```

Result

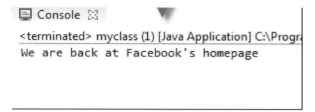

Part 2) Reading a Table

There are times when we need to access elements (usually texts) that are within HTML tables. However, it is very seldom for a web designer to provide an id or name attribute to a certain cell in the table. Therefore, we cannot use the usual methods such as "By.id()", "By.name()", or "By.cssSelector()". In this case, the most reliable option is to access them using the "By.xpath()" method.

XPath Syntax

Consider the HTML code below.

```
<html>
    <head>
        <title>Sample</title>
    </head>
    <body>
        <table border="1">
            <tbody>
                <tr>
                    <td>first cell</td>
                    <td>second cell</td>
                </tr>
                <tr>
                    <td>third cell</td>
                    <td>fourth cell</td>
                </tr>
            </tbody>
        </table>
    </body>
</html>
```

We will use XPath to get the inner text of the cell containing the text "fourth cell."

we will try to
access this cell

Step 1 - Set the Parent Element (table)

XPath locators in WebDriver always start with a double forward slash "//" and then followed by the parent element. Since we are dealing with tables, the parent element should always be the <table> tag. The first portion of our XPath locator should, therefore, start with "//table".

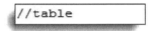

Step 2 - Add the child elements

The element immediately under <table> is <tbody> so we can say that <tbody> is the "child" of <table>. And also, <table> is the "parent" of <tbody>. All child elements in XPath are placed to the right of their parent element, separated with one forward slash "/" like the code shown below.

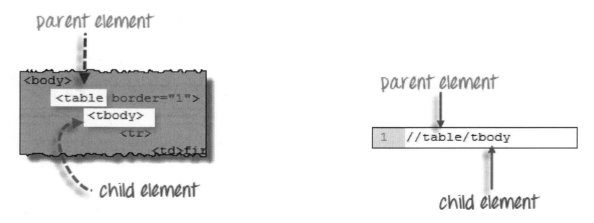

Step 3 - Add Predicates

The <tbody> element contains two <tr> tags. We can now say that these two <tr> tags are "children" of <tbody>. Consequently, we can say that <tbody> is the parent of both the <tr> elements.

Another thing we can conclude is that the two <tr> elements are siblings. **Siblings refer to child elements having the same parent**.

To get to the <td> we wish to access (the one with the text "fourth cell"), we must first access the **second** <tr> and not the first. If we simply write "//table/tbody/tr", then we will be accessing the first <tr> tag.

So, how do we access the second <tr> then? The answer to this is to use **Predicates**.

Predicates are numbers or HTML attributes enclosed in a pair of square brackets "[ ]" that distinguish a child element from its siblings. Since the <tr> we need to access is the second one, we shall use "[2]" as the predicate.

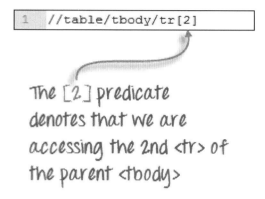

The [2] predicate denotes that we are accessing the 2nd <tr> of the parent <tbody>

If we won't use any predicate, XPath will access the first sibling. Therefore, we can access the first <tr> using either of these XPath codes.

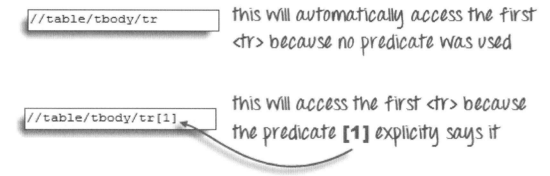

this will automatically access the first <tr> because no predicate was used

this will access the first <tr> because the predicate **[1]** explicitly says it

Step 4 - Add the Succeeding Child Elements Using the Appropriate Predicates

The next element we need to access is the second <td>. Applying the principles we have learned from steps 2 and 3, we will finalize our XPath code to be like the one shown below.

```
//table/tbody/tr[2]/td[2]
```

Now that we have the correct XPath locator, we can already access the cell that we wanted to and obtain its inner text using the code below. It assumes that you have saved the HTML code above as "newhtml.html" within your C Drive.

```
    public static void main(String[] args) {
        String baseUrl = "file:///C:/newhtml.html";
        WebDriver driver = new FirefoxDriver();

        driver.get(baseUrl);
        String innerText = driver.findElement(
                By.xpath("//table/tbody/tr[2]/td[2]")).getText();
        System.out.println(innerText);
        driver.quit();
    }
}
```

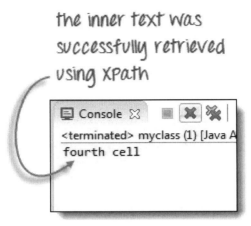

the inner text was
successfully retrieved
using XPath

Accessing Nested Tables

The same principles discussed above applies to nested tables. **Nested tables are tables located within another table**. An example is shown below.

```html
<html>
    <head>
        <title>Sample</title>
    </head>
    <body>
        <!--outer table-->
        <table border="1">
            <tbody>
                <tr>
                    <td>ONE</td>
                    <td>TWO</td>
                </tr>
                <tr>
                    <td>THREE</td>
                    <td>
                        <!--inner table-->
                        <table border="1">
                            <tbody>
                                <tr>
                                    <td>1-2-3</td>
                                    <td>4-5-6</td>
                                </tr>
                                <tr>
                                    <td>7-8-9</td>
                                    <td>10-11-12</td>
                                </tr>
                            </tbody>
                        </table>
                    </td>
                </tr>
            </tbody>
        </table>
    </body>
</html>
```

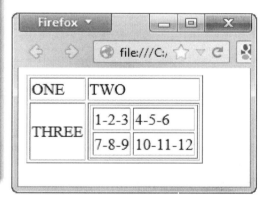

To access the cell with the text "4-5-6" using the "//parent/child" and predicate concepts from the previous section, we should be able to come up with the XPath code below.

The outer table

The inner table

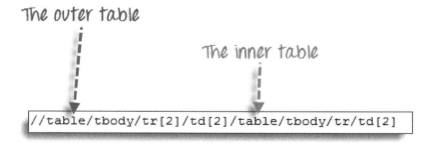

```
//table/tbody/tr[2]/td[2]/table/tbody/tr/td[2]
```

The WebDriver code below should be able to retrieve the inner text of the cell which we are accessing.

```
public static void main(String[] args) {
    String baseUrl = "file:///C:/newhtml.html";
    WebDriver driver = new FirefoxDriver();

    driver.get(baseUrl);
    String innerText = driver.findElement(By
            .xpath("//table/tbody/tr[2]/td[2]/table/tbody/tr/td[2]"))
            .getText();
    System.out.println(innerText);
    driver.quit();
}
```

The output below confirms that the inner table was successfully accessed.

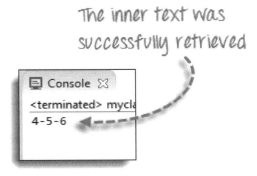

The inner text was
successfully retrieved

Using Attributes as Predicates

If the element is written deep within the HTML code such that the number to use for the predicate is very difficult to determine, we can use that element's unique attribute instead.

In the example below, the "New York to Chicago" cell is located deep into Mercury Tours homepage's HTML code.

Specials	
Atlanta to Las Vegas	$398
Boston to San Francisco	$513
Los Angeles to Chicago	$168
New York to Chicago	$198
Phoenix to San Francisco	$213

```
⊟ <body>
    ⊟ <div>
        ⊟ <table height="100%" cellspacing="0" cellpadding="0" border="0">
            ⊟ <tbody>
                ⊟ <tr>
                    ⊞ <td valign="top" bgcolor="#003366">
                    ⊟ <td valign="top">
                        ⊟ <table cellspacing="0" cellpadding="0" border="0">
                            ⊟ <tbody>
                                ⊞ <tr>
                                ⊞ <tr>
                                ⊞ <tr>
                                ⊟ <tr>
                                    ⊟ <td>
                                        ⊟ <table cellspacing="0" cellpadding="0" border="0">
                                            ⊟ <tbody>
                                                ⊟ <tr>
                                                    <td width="14"> </td>
                                                ⊟ <td>
                                                    ⊟ <table width="492" cellspacing="0" cellpadding="0" borde
                                                        ⊟ <tbody>
                                                            <tr> </tr>
                                                            ⊟ <tr>
                                                                ⊟ <td width="273" valign="top">
                                                                    ⊞ <p>
                                                                    ⊟ <table width="100%" cellspacing="0" cellpa
                                                                        ⊟ <tbody>
                                                                            ⊞ <tr>
                                                                            ⊞ <tr>
                                                                            ⊟ <tr valign="top">
                                                                                ⊟ <td height="101">
                                                                                    ⊟ <table width="270" cellspac
                                                                                        ⊟ <tbody>
                                                                                            ⊟ <tr bgcolor="#CCCCCC
                                                                                                ⊟ <td width="80%">
                                                                                                    <font size="2
                                                                                                    Vegas </font>
                                                                                            </td>
                                                                                    ⊞ <td width="20%">
```

this is the <table> that holds the New York to Chicago cell. Notice that it is burried deep into the HTML code, and the number to use as predicate is difficult to determine.

In this case, we can use the table's unique attribute (width="270") as the predicate. **Attributes are used as predicates by prefixing them with the @ symbol**. In the example above, the "New York to Chicago" cell is located in the first <td> of the fourth <tr>, and so our XPath should be as shown below.

```
//table[@width="270"]/tbody/tr[4]/td
```

Remember that when we put the XPath code in Java, we should use the escape character backward slash "\" for the double quotation marks on both sides of "270" so that the string argument of By.xpath() will not be terminated prematurely.

```
By.xpath("//table[@width=\"270\"]/tbody/tr[4]/td"))
```

use the escape characters here

We are now ready to access that cell using the code below.

```java
public static void main(String[] args) {
    String baseUrl = "http://newtours.demoaut.com/";
    WebDriver driver = new FirefoxDriver();

    driver.get(baseUrl);
    String innerText = driver.findElement(By
            .xpath("//table[@width=\"270\"]/tbody/tr[4]/td"))
            .getText();
    System.out.println(innerText);
    driver.quit();
}
```

the inner text was
successfully retrieved.

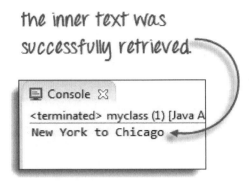

Shortcut: Use Firebug for Accessing Tables in Selenium

If the number or attribute of an element is extremely difficult or impossible to obtain, the quickest way to generate the XPath code is thru Firebug.

Consider the example below from Mercury Tours homepage.

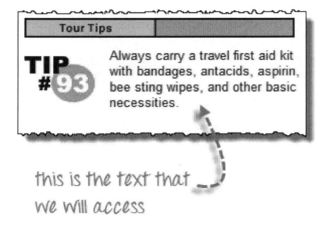

this is the text that
we will access

Step 1

Use Firebug to obtain the XPath code.

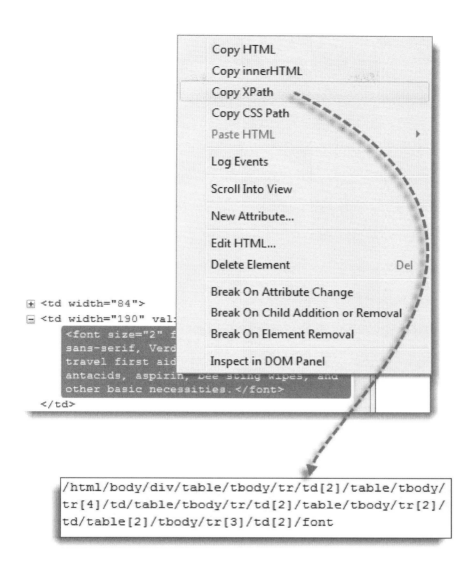

Step 2

Look for the first "table" parent element and delete everything to the left of it.

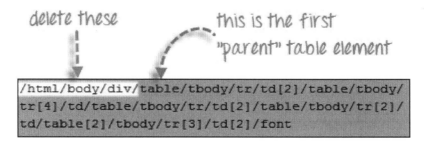

Step 3

Prefix the remaining portion of the code with double forward slash "//" and copy it over to your WebDriver code.

The remaining portion of the code, trimmed and prefixed with "//"

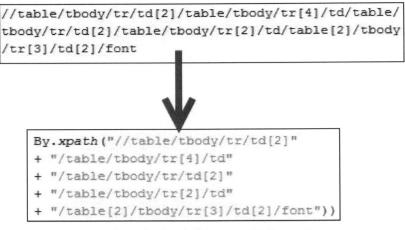

```
//table/tbody/tr/td[2]/table/tbody/tr[4]/td/table/
tbody/tr/td[2]/table/tbody/tr[2]/td/table[2]/tbody
/tr[3]/td[2]/font
```

```
By.xpath("//table/tbody/tr/td[2]"
+ "/table/tbody/tr[4]/td"
+ "/table/tbody/tr/td[2]"
+ "/table/tbody/tr[2]/td"
+ "/table[2]/tbody/tr[3]/td[2]/font"))
```

when pasted onto the By.xpath() method

The WebDriver code below will be able to successfully retrieve the inner text of the element we are accessing.

```java
public static void main(String[] args) {
    String baseUrl = "http://newtours.demoaut.com/";
    WebDriver driver = new FirefoxDriver();

    driver.get(baseUrl);
    String innerText = driver.findElement(
            By.xpath("//table/tbody/tr/td[2]"
            + "/table/tbody/tr[4]/td"
            + "/table/tbody/tr/td[2]"
            + "/table/tbody/tr[2]/td"
            + "/table[2]/tbody/tr[3]/td[2]/font"))
            .getText();
    System.out.println(innerText);
    driver.quit();
}
```

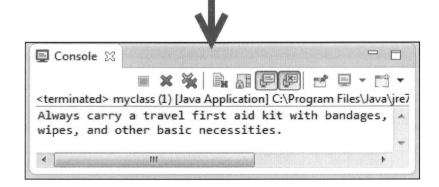

Console ☒

<terminated> myclass (1) [Java Application] C:\Program Files\Java\jre7

Always carry a travel first aid kit with bandages, wipes, and other basic necessities.

Summary

- Accessing links using their exact match is done using By.linkText() method.

- Accessing links using their partial match is done using By.partialLinkText() method.

- If there are multiple matches, By.linkText() and By.partialLinkText() will only select the first match.

- Pattern matching using By.linkText() and By.partialLinkText() is case-sensitive.

- The By.tagName("a") method is used to fetch all links within a page.

- Links can be accessed by the By.linkText() and By.partialLinkText() whether they are inside or outside block-level elements.

- Accessing image links are done using By.cssSelector() and By.xpath() methods.

- By.xpath() is commonly used to access table elements.

Chapter 12: Keyboard Mouse Events, Uploading Files - Webdriver

In this tutorial, we will learn handling Keyboard and Mouse Event in Selenium Webdriver

Handling Keyboard & Mouse Events

Handling special keyboard and mouse events are done using the **Advanced User Interactions API**. It contains the **Actions** and the **Action** classes that are needed when executing these events. The following are the most commonly used keyboard and mouse events provided by the Actions class.

Method	Description
clickAndHold()	Clicks (without releasing) at the current mouse location.
contextClick()	Performs a context-click at the current mouse location.
doubleClick()	Performs a double-click at the current

	mouse location.
dragAndDrop(source, target)	Performs click-and-hold at the location of the source element, moves to the location of the target element, then releases the mouse. **Parameters:** source- element to emulate button down at. target- element to move to and release the mouse at.
dragAndDropBy(source, x-offset, y-offset)	Performs click-and-hold at the location of the source element, moves by a given offset, then releases the mouse. **Parameters**: source- element to emulate button down at. xOffset- horizontal move offset. yOffset- vertical move offset.
keyDown(modifier_key)	Performs a modifier key press. Does not release the modifier key - subsequent interactions may assume it's kept pressed. **Parameters**: modifier_key - any of the modifier keys (Keys.ALT, Keys.SHIFT, or Keys.CONTROL)
keyUp(modifier _key)	Performs a key release.

	Parameters: modifier_key - any of the modifier keys (Keys.ALT, Keys.SHIFT, or Keys.CONTROL)
moveByOffset(x-offset, y-offset)	Moves the mouse from its current position (or 0,0) by the given offset. **Parameters**: x-offset- horizontal offset. A negative value means moving the mouse left. y-offset- vertical offset. A negative value means moving the mouse up.
moveToElement(toElement)	Moves the mouse to the middle of the element. **Parameters**: toElement- element to move to.
release()	Releases the depressed left mouse button at the current mouse location
sendKeys(onElement, charsequence)	Sends a series of keystrokes onto the element. **Parameters**: onElement - element that will receive the keystrokes, usually a text field charsequence - any string value representing the sequence of keystrokes to be sent

In the following example, we shall use the moveToElement() method to mouse-over on one Mercury Tours' table rows. See the example below.

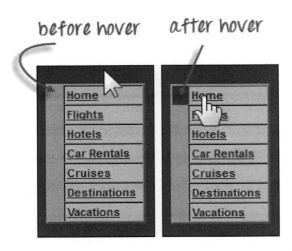

before hover   after hover

The cell shown above is a portion of a <TR> element. If not hovered, its color is #FFC455 (orange). After hovering, the cell's color becomes transparent. It becomes the same color as the blue background of the whole orange table.

Step 1: Import the **Actions** and **Action** classes.

```
import org.openqa.selenium.interactions.Action;
import org.openqa.selenium.interactions.Actions;
```

Step 2: Instantiate a new Actions object.

```
Actions builder = new Actions(driver);
```

Step 3: Instantiate an Action using the Actions object in step 2.

```
Action mouseOverHome = builder
        .moveToElement(link_Home)
        .build();
```

In this case, we are going to use the moveToElement() method because we are simply going to mouse-over the "Home" link. The build() method is always the final method used so that all the listed actions will be compiled into a single step.

Step 4: Use the perform() method when executing the Action object we designed in Step 3.

```
mouseOverHome.perform();
```

Below is the whole WebDriver code to check the background color of the <TR> element before and after the mouse-over.

```
package newproject;

import org.openqa.selenium.*;
import org.openqa.selenium.firefox.FirefoxDriver;
import org.openqa.selenium.interactions.Action;
import org.openqa.selenium.interactions.Actions;
```

```java
public class PG7 {

    public static void main(String[] args) {
        String baseUrl = "http://newtours.demoaut.com/";
        System.setProperty("webdriver.firefox.marionette","C:\\geckodriver.exe");
            WebDriver driver = new FirefoxDriver();


            driver.get(baseUrl);
            WebElement link_Home = driver.findElement(By.linkText("Home"));
            WebElement td_Home = driver
                    .findElement(By
                    .xpath("//html/body/div"
                    + "/table/tbody/tr/td"
                    + "/table/tbody/tr/td"
                    + "/table/tbody/tr/td"
                    + "/table/tbody/tr"));

            Actions builder = new Actions(driver);
            Action mouseOverHome = builder
                    .moveToElement(link_Home)
                    .build();

            String bgColor = td_Home.getCssValue("background-color");
            System.out.println("Before hover: " + bgColor);
            mouseOverHome.perform();
            bgColor = td_Home.getCssValue("background-color");
            System.out.println("After hover: " + bgColor);
            driver.close();
    }
}
```

The output below clearly states that the background color became transparent after the mouse-over.

Console ⌧
<terminated> myclass (1) [Java Application] C:\Program
Before hover: rgba(255, 165, 0, 1)
After hover: transparent

Building a Series of Multiple Actions

You can build a series of actions using the Action and Actions classes. Just remember to close the series with the build() method. Consider the sample code below.

```java
public static void main(String[] args) {
    String baseUrl = "http://www.facebook.com/";
    WebDriver driver = new FirefoxDriver();

    driver.get(baseUrl);
    WebElement txtUsername = driver.findElement(By.id("email"));

    Actions builder = new Actions(driver);
    Action seriesOfActions = builder
        .moveToElement(txtUsername)
        .click()
        .keyDown(txtUsername, Keys.SHIFT)         // this will type "hello" in uppercase
        .sendKeys(txtUsername, "hello")
        .keyUp(txtUsername, Keys.SHIFT)
        .doubleClick(txtUsername)                  // this will highlight the text "HELLO"
        .contextClick()                            // this will bring up the context menu
        .build();

    seriesOfActions.perform();
}
```

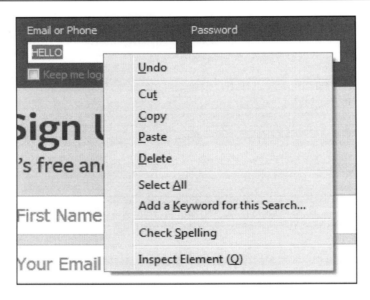

Summary

- Handling special keyboard and mouse events are done using the AdvancedUserInteractions API.

- Frequently used Keyword and Mouse Events are doubleClick(), keyUp, dragAndDropBy, contextClick & sendKeys.

Chapter 13: How TestNG makes Selenium tests easier

What is TestNG?

So far we had been doing Selenium tests without generating a proper format for the test results. From this point on, we shall tackle how to make these reports using a test framework called TestNG.

TestNG is a **Testing** framework that overcomes the limitations of another popular testing framework called JUnit. The "NG" means "Next Generation." Most Selenium users use this more than **Junit** because of its advantages. There are so many features of TestNG, but we will only focus on the most important ones that we can use in Selenium.

Advantages of TestNG over JUnit

There are three major advantages of TestNG over JUnit:

- Annotations are easier to understand
- Test cases can be grouped more easily
- Parallel testing is possible

Annotations in TestNG are lines of code that can control how the method below them will be executed. They are always preceded by the @ symbol. A very early and quick example is the one shown below.

These are 2 examples of annotations

```
@Test(priority = 0)
public void goToHomepage() {
    driver.get(baseUrl);
    Assert.assertEquals(driver.getTitle(), "Welcome: Mercury Tours");
}

@Test(priority = 1)
public void logout() {
    driver.findElement(By.linkText("SIGN-OFF")).click();
    Assert.assertEquals("Sign-on: Mercury Tours", driver.getTitle());
}
```

The example above simply says that the method goToHomepage() should be executed first before logout() because it has a lower priority number

Annotations will be discussed later in the section named "Annotations used in TestNG," so it is perfectly ok if you do not understand the above example just yet. It is just important to note for now that annotations in TestNG are easier to code and understand than in JUnit.

The ability to run tests in parallel is available in TestNG but not in JUnit, so it is the more preferred framework of testers using Selenium Grid.

Why do we need TestNG in Selenium?

TestNG can generate reports based on our Selenium test results.

- WebDriver has no native mechanism for generating reports.

- TestNG can generate the report in a readable format like the one shown below.

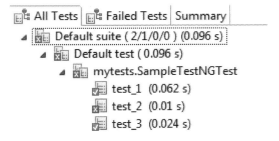

TestNG simplifies the way the tests are coded

- There is no more need for a static main method in our tests. The sequence of actions is regulated by easy-to-understand annotations that do not require methods to be static.

```java
public class myclass {

    public static String baseUrl = "http://newtours.demoaut.com/";
    public static WebDriver driver = new FirefoxDriver();

    public static void main(String[] args) {
        driver.get(baseUrl);
        verifyHomepageTitle();
        driver.quit();
    }

    public static void verifyHomepageTitle() {
        String expectedTitle = "Welcome: Mercury Tours";
        String actualTitle = driver.getTitle();
        try {
            Assert.assertEquals(actualTitle, expectedTitle);
            System.out.println("Test Passed");
        } catch (Throwable e) {
            System.out.println("Test Failed");
        }
    }
}
```

Usual structure (somewhat difficult to read)

```java
public class SampleTestNGTest {
    public String baseUrl = "http://newtours.demoaut.com/";
    public WebDriver driver;

    @BeforeTest
    public void setBaseURL() {
        driver = new FirefoxDriver();
        driver.get(baseUrl);
    }

    @Test
    public void verifyHomepageTitle() {
        String expectedTitle = "Welcome: Mercury Tours";
        String actualTitle = driver.getTitle();
        Assert.assertEquals(actualTitle, expectedTitle);
    }


    @AfterTest
    public void endSession() {
        driver.quit();
    }
}
```

- Uncaught exceptions are automatically handled by TestNG without terminating the test prematurely. These exceptions are reported as failed steps in the report.

Installing TestNG in Eclipse

Step 1:

- Launch Eclipse.
- On the menu bar, click Help.
- Choose the "Eclipse Marketplace..." option.

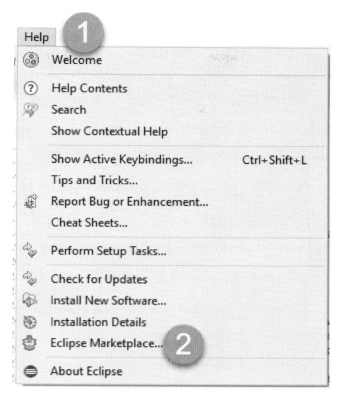

Step 2: In the Eclipse Marketplace dialog box, type TestNG in the search box and press the search button(magnifying glass) or press enter key

Step 3: Click Install

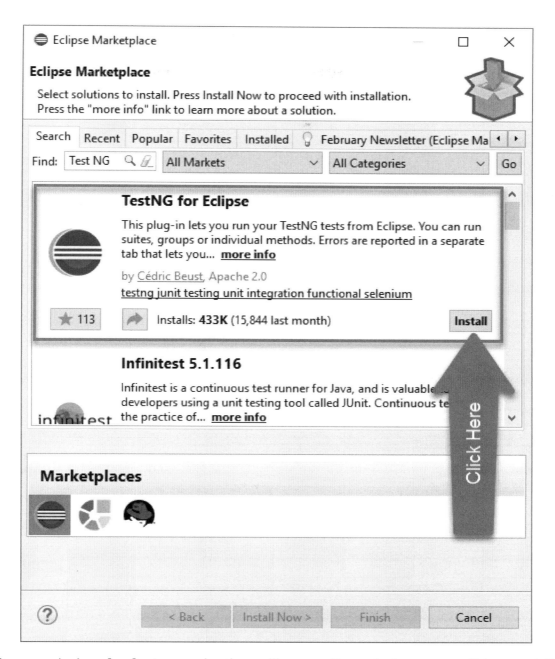

Step 4: A new window for feature selection will open, Do not change anything and Click on confirm button

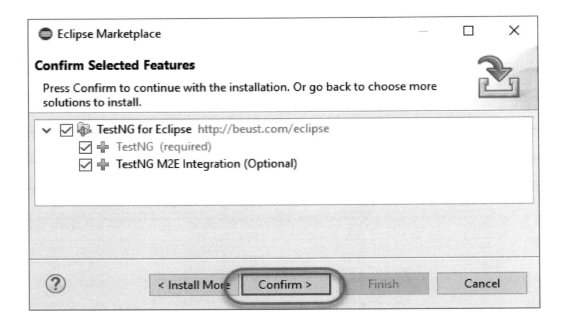

Step 5:

- Click Next again on the succeeding dialog box until you reach the License Agreement dialog.

- Click "I accept the terms of the license agreement" then click Finish.

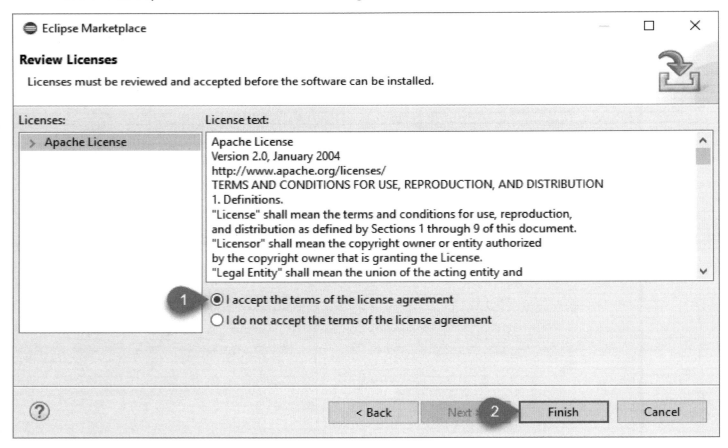

Step 6: If you encounter a Security warning, just click OK

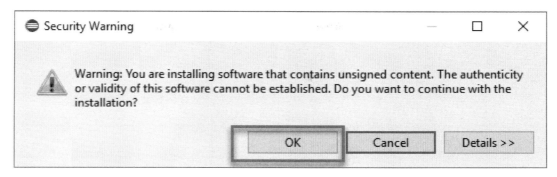

Wait for the installation to finish

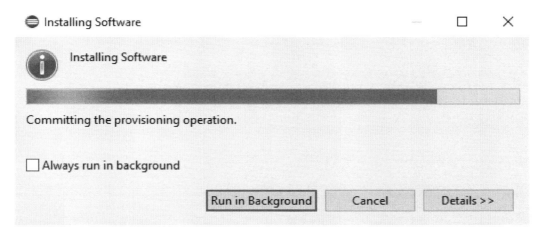

Step 7: When Eclipse prompts you for a restart, just click Yes.

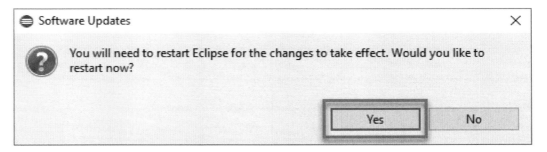

Step 8: After the restart, verify if TestNG was indeed successfully installed. Click Window > Preferences and see if TestNG is included on the Preferences list.

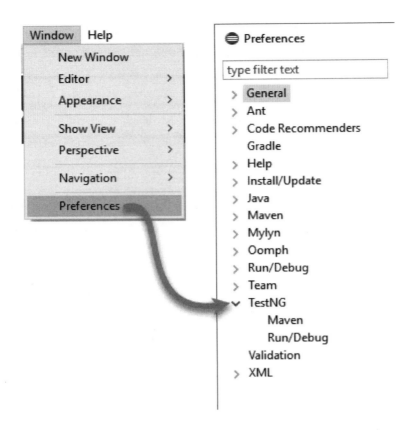

First test case using annotations

Before we create a test case, we should first setup a new TestNG Project in Eclipse and name it as "FirstTestNGProject".

Setting up a new TestNG Project

Step 1: Click File > New > **Java** Project

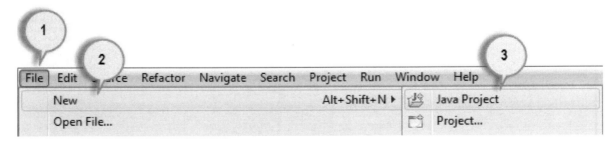

Step 2: Type "FirstTestNGProject" as the Project Name then click Next.

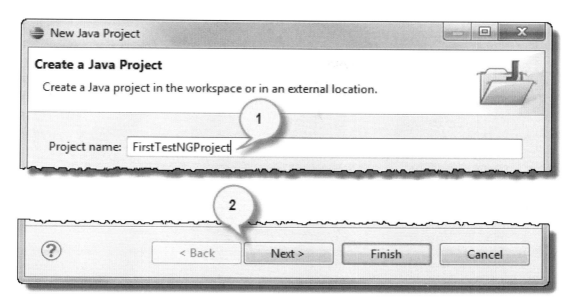

Step 3: We will now start to import the TestNG Libraries onto our project. Click on the "Libraries" tab, and then "Add Library…"

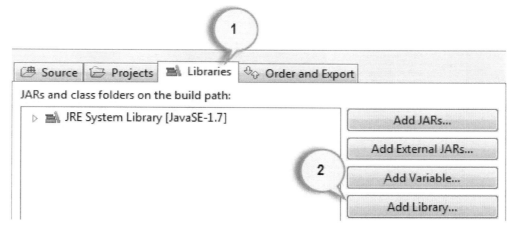

Step 4: On the Add Library dialog, choose "TestNG" and click Next.

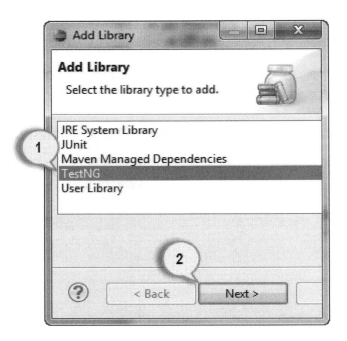

Step 5: Click Finish.

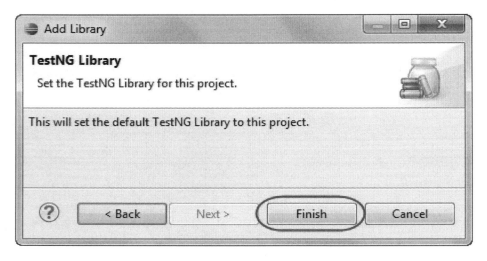

You should notice that TestNG is included on the Libraries list.

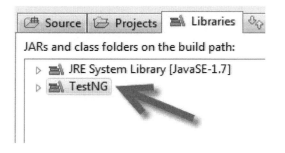

Step 6: We will now add the JAR files that contain the Selenium API. These files are found in the Java client driver that we downloaded from **http://docs.seleniumhq.org/download/** when we were installing Selenium and Eclipse in the previous chapters.

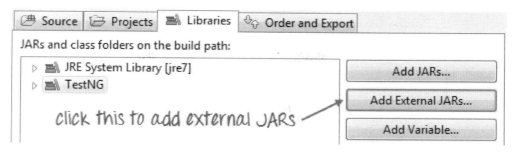

Then, navigate to where you have placed the Selenium JAR files.

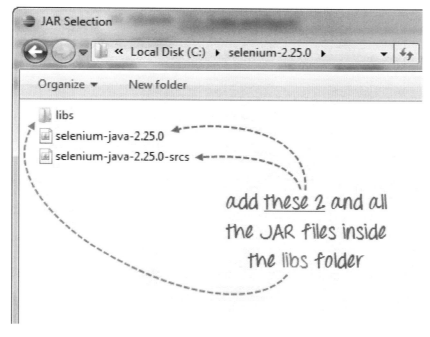

After adding the external JARs, your screen should look like this.

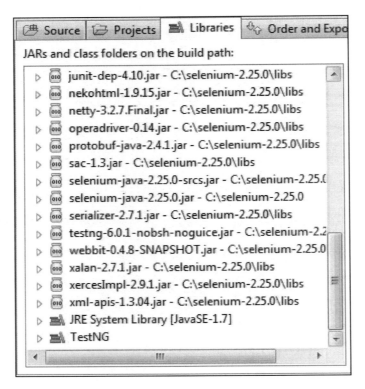

Step 7: Click Finish and verify that our FirstTestNGProject is visible on Eclipse's Package Explorer window.

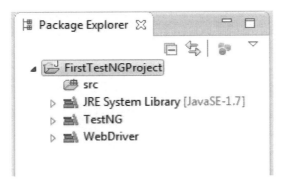

Creating a New TestNG Test File

Now that we are done setting up our project, let us create a new TestNG file.

Step 1: Right-click on the "src" package folder then choose New > Other…

Step 2: Click on the TestNG folder and select the "TestNG class" option. Click Next.

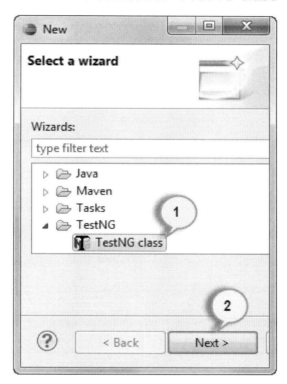

Step 3: Type the values indicated below on the appropriate input boxes and click Finish. Notice that we have named our Java file as "FirstTestNGFile".

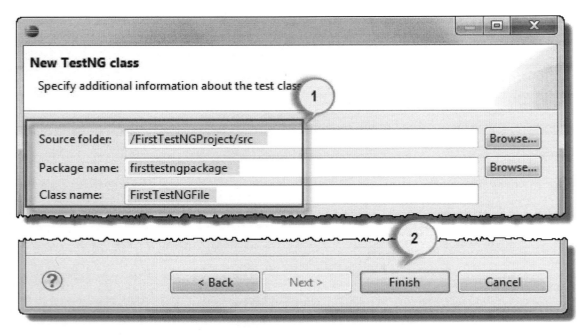

Eclipse should automatically create the template for our TestNG file shown below.

```
FirstTestNGFile.java ⊠
▶ 📁 FirstTestNGProject ▶ 🗂 src ▶ ⊞ firsttestngp
 1  package firsttestngpackage;
 2
 3  import org.testng.annotations.Test;
 4
 5  public class FirstTestNGFile {
 6⊖   @Test
 7     public void f() {
 8     }
 9  }
10
```

Coding Our First Test Case

Let us now create our first test case that will check if Mercury Tours' homepage is correct. Type your code as shown below.

```java
package firsttestngpackage;
import org.openqa.selenium.*;
import org.openqa.selenium.firefox.FirefoxDriver;
import org.testng.Assert;
import org.testng.annotations.*;

public class firsttestngfile {
    public String baseUrl = "http://newtours.demoaut.com/";
    String driverPath = "C:\\geckodriver.exe";
    public WebDriver driver ;
```

```
@Test
public void verifyHomepageTitle() {

    System.out.println("launching firefox browser");
    System.setProperty("webdriver.firefox.marionette", driverPath);
    driver = new FirefoxDriver();
    driver.get(baseUrl);
    String expectedTitle = "Welcome: Mercury Tours";
    String actualTitle = driver.getTitle();
    Assert.assertEquals(actualTitle, expectedTitle);
    driver.close();
  }
}
```

Notice the following.

- TestNG does not require you to have a main() method.

- Methods need not be static.

- We used the @Test annotation. **@Test is used to tell that the method under it is a test case**. In this case, we have set the verifyHomepageTitle() method to be our test case, so we placed an '@Test' annotation above it.

- Since we use annotations in TestNG, we needed to import the package org.testng.annotations.*.

- We used the Assert class. **The Assert class is used to conduct verification operations in TestNG**. To use it, we need to import the org.testng.Assert package.

You may have multiple test cases (therefore, multiple @Test annotations) in a single TestNG file. This will be tackled in more detail later in the section "Annotations used in TestNG."

Running the Test

To run the test, simply run the file in Eclipse as you normally do. Eclipse will provide two outputs – one in the Console window and the other on the TestNG Results window.

TestNG Results Window

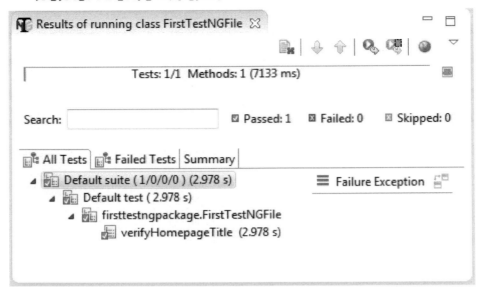

Console Window

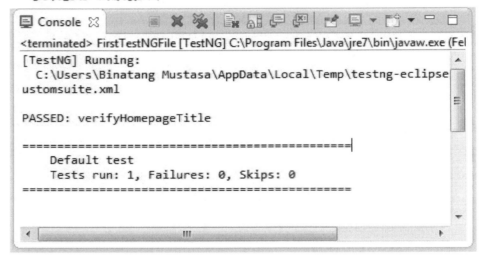

Checking reports created by TestNG

The Console window in Eclipse gives a text-based report of our test case results while the TestNG Results window gives us a graphical one.

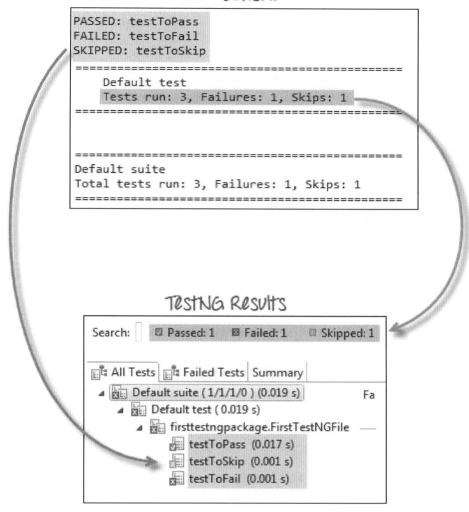

Console

```
PASSED: testToPass
FAILED: testToFail
SKIPPED: testToSkip

===============================================
    Default test
    Tests run: 3, Failures: 1, Skips: 1
===============================================



===============================================
Default suite
Total tests run: 3, Failures: 1, Skips: 1
===============================================
```

TestNG Results

Search: ☑ Passed: 1   ☒ Failed: 1   ☐ Skipped: 1

All Tests | Failed Tests | Summary

⊿ Default suite (1/1/1/0) (0.019 s)   Fa
  ⊿ Default test (0.019 s)
    ⊿ firsttestngpackage.FirstTestNGFile ——
        testToPass (0.017 s)
        testToSkip (0.001 s)
        testToFail (0.001 s)

Generating HTML Reports

TestNG has the ability to generate reports in HTML format.

Step 1: After running our FirstTestNGFile that we created in the previous section, right-click the project name (FirstTestNGProject) in the Project Explorer window then click on the "Refresh" option.

Step 2: Notice that a "test-output" folder was created. Expand it and look for an index.html file. This HTML file is a report of the results of the most recent test run.

Step 3: Double-click on that index.html file to open it within Eclipse's built-in web browser. You can refresh this page any time after you rerun your test by simply pressing F5 just like in ordinary web browsers.

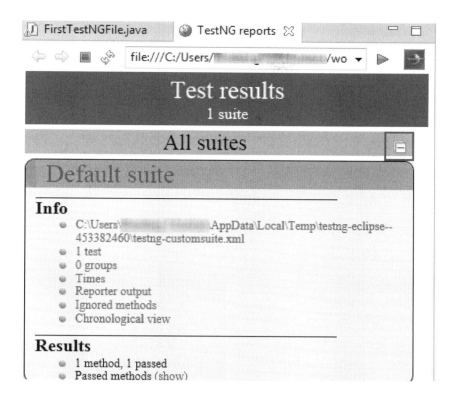

Annotations used in TestNG

In the previous section, you have been introduced to the @Test annotation. Now, we shall be studying more advanced annotations and their usages.

Multiple Test Cases

We can use multiple @Test annotations in a single TestNG file. By default, methods annotated by @Test are executed alphabetically. See the code below. Though the methods c_test, a_test, and b_test are not arranged alphabetically in the code, they will be executed as such.

```
public class FirstTestNGFile {

    @Test
    public void c_test() {
        Assert.fail();
    }

    @Test
    public void a_test() {
        Assert.assertTrue(true);
    }

    @Test
    public void b_test() {
        throw new SkipException("Skipping b_test...");
    }
}
```

Run this code and on the generated index.html page, click "Chronological view."

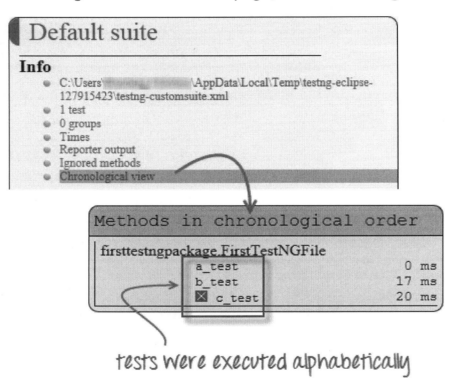

tests were executed alphabetically

Parameters

If you want the methods to be executed in a different order, use the parameter "priority". **Parameters are keywords that modify the annotation's function**.

- Parameters require you to assign a value to them. You do.this by placing a "=" next to them, and then followed by the value.

- Parameters are enclosed in a pair of parentheses which are placed right after the annotation like the code snippet shown below.

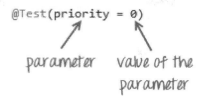

TestNG will execute the @Test annotation with the lowest priority value up to the largest. There is no need for your priority values to be consecutive.

```
public class FirstTestNGFile {

    @Test(priority = 3)          ───── the 2nd least priority value so
    public void c_test() {              this will be executed 2nd
        Assert.fail();
    }

    @Test(priority = 0)          ───── this has the lowest priority value
    public void a_test() {              so this will be executed first
        Assert.assertTrue(true);
    }

    @Test(priority = 7)          ───── largest priority value so this will
    public void b_test() {              be executed last
        throw new SkipException("Skipping b_test...");
    }
}
```

The TestNG HTML report will confirm that the methods were executed based on the ascending value of priority.

Methods in chronological order	
firsttestngpackage.FirstTestNGFile	
a_test	0 ms
☒ c_test	18 ms
b_test	23 ms

Multiple Parameters

Aside from "priority," @Test has another parameter called "alwaysRun" which can only be set to either "true" or "false." **To use two or more parameters in a single annotation, separate them with a comma** such as the one shown below.

```
@Test(priority = 0, enabled = true)
```

@BeforeTest and @AfterTest

@BeforeTest	methods under this annotation will be executed **prior to the first test case in the TestNG file**.

@AfterTest	methods under this annotation will be executed **after all test cases in the TestNG file are executed**.

Consider the code below.

```
package firsttestngpackage;
import org.openqa.selenium.*;
import org.openqa.selenium.firefox.FirefoxDriver;
import org.testng.Assert;
import org.testng.annotations.*;
public class firsttestngfile {
    public String baseUrl = "http://newtours.demoaut.com/";
    String driverPath = "C:\\geckodriver.exe";
    public WebDriver driver ;

    @BeforeTest
    public void launchBrowser() {
        System.out.println("launching firefox browser");
        System.setProperty("webdriver.firefox.marionette", driverPath);
        driver = new FirefoxDriver();
        driver.get(baseUrl);
    }
    @Test
    public void verifyHomepageTitle() {
```

```
        String expectedTitle = "Welcome: Mercury Tours";
        String actualTitle = driver.getTitle();
        Assert.assertEquals(actualTitle, expectedTitle);
    }
    @AfterTest
    public void terminateBrowser(){
        driver.close();
    }
}
```

Applying the logic presented by the table and the code above, we can predict that the sequence by which methods will be executed is:

- 1st - launchBrowser()

- 2nd - verifyHomepageTitle()

- 3rd - terminateBrowser()

The placement of the annotation blocks can be interchanged without affecting the chronological order by which they will be executed. For example, try to rearrange the annotation blocks such that your code would look similar to the one below.

```
package firsttestngpackage;
import org.openqa.selenium.*;
import org.openqa.selenium.firefox.FirefoxDriver;
import org.testng.Assert;
import org.testng.annotations.*;
public class firsttestngfile {
    public String baseUrl = "http://newtours.demoaut.com/";
    String driverPath = "C:\\geckodriver.exe";
    public WebDriver driver ;
    @AfterTest                          //Jumbled
    public void terminateBrowser(){
        driver.close();
    }
    @BeforeTest                         //Jumbled
    public void launchBrowser() {
        System.out.println("launching firefox browser");
        System.setProperty("webdriver.firefox.marionette", driverPath);
        driver = new FirefoxDriver();
        driver.get(baseUrl);
    }
    @Test                               //Jumbled
    public void verifyHomepageTitle() {
        String expectedTitle = "Welcome: Mercury Tours";
        String actualTitle = driver.getTitle();
        Assert.assertEquals(actualTitle, expectedTitle);
```

```
        }

    }
}
```
Run the code above and notice that

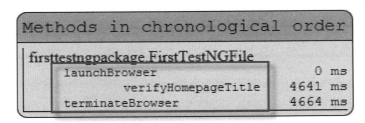

@BeforeMethod and @AfterMethod

@BeforeMethod	methods under this annotation will be executed **prior to each method in each test case**.

@AfterMethod	methods under this annotation will be executed **after each method in each test case.**

In Mercury Tours, suppose we like to verify the titles of the target pages of the two links below.

The flow of our test would be:

- Go to the homepage and verify its title.

- Click REGISTER and verify the title of its target page.

- Go back to the homepage and verify if it still has the correct title.

- Click SUPPORT and verify the title of its target page.

- Go back to the homepage and verify if it still has the correct title.

The code below illustrates how @BeforeMethod and @AfterMethod are used to efficiently execute the scenario mentioned above.

```
package firsttestngpackage;
import org.openqa.selenium.*;
import org.openqa.selenium.firefox.FirefoxDriver;
import org.testng.Assert;
import org.testng.annotations.*;
@Test
```

```java
public class firsttestngfile {
    public String baseUrl = "http://newtours.demoaut.com/";
    String driverPath = "C:\\geckodriver.exe";
    public WebDriver driver;
    public String expected = null;
    public String actual = null;
        @BeforeTest
      public void launchBrowser() {
          System.out.println("launching firefox browser");
          System.setProperty("webdriver.firefox.marionette", driverPath);
          driver= new FirefoxDriver();
          driver.get(baseUrl);
      }

    @BeforeMethod
    public void verifyHomepageTitle() {
        String expectedTitle = "Welcome: Mercury Tours";
        String actualTitle = driver.getTitle();
        Assert.assertEquals(actualTitle, expectedTitle);
    }

        @Test(priority = 0)
    public void register(){
        driver.findElement(By.linkText("REGISTER")).click() ;
        expected = "Register: Mercury Tours";
        actual = driver.getTitle();
        Assert.assertEquals(actual, expected);
    }

        @Test(priority = 1)
    public void support() {
          driver.findElement(By.linkText("SUPPORT")).click() ;
          expected = "Under Construction: Mercury Tours";
          actual = driver.getTitle();
          Assert.assertEquals(actual, expected);
    }
    @AfterMethod
    public void goBackToHomepage ( ) {
          driver.findElement(By.linkText("Home")).click() ;
    }

    @AfterTest
    public void terminateBrowser(){
        driver.close();
    }
}
```

After executing this test, your TestNG should report the following sequence.

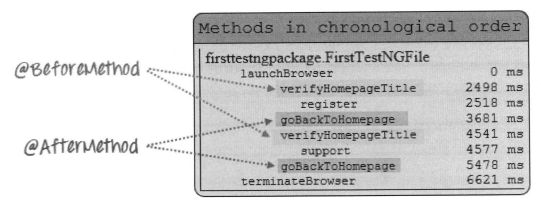

Simply put, @BeforeMethod should contain methods that you need to run **before** each test case while @AfterMethod should contain methods that you need to run **after** each test case.

Summary of TestNG Annotations

@BeforeSuite: The annotated method will be run before all tests in this suite have run.

@AfterSuite: The annotated method will be run after all tests in this suite have run.

@BeforeTest: The annotated method will be run before any test method belonging to the classes inside the tag is run.

@AfterTest: The annotated method will be run after all the test methods belonging to the classes inside the tag have run.

@BeforeGroups: The list of groups that this configuration method will run before. This method is guaranteed to run shortly before the first test method that belongs to any of these groups is invoked.

@AfterGroups: The list of groups that this configuration method will run after. This method is guaranteed to run shortly after the last test method that belongs to any of these groups is invoked.

@BeforeClass: The annotated method will be run before the first test method in the current class is invoked.

@AfterClass: The annotated method will be run after all the test methods in the current class have been run.

@BeforeMethod: The annotated method will be run before each test method.

@AfterMethod: The annotated method will be run after each test method.

@Test: The annotated method is a part of a test case

Conclusion

- TestNG is a testing framework that is capable of making Selenium tests easier to understand and of generating reports that are easy to understand.

- The main advantages of TestNG over JUnit are the following.

  - Annotations are easier to use and understand.

  - Test cases can be grouped more easily.

  - TestNG allows us to create parallel tests.

- The Console window in Eclipse generates a text-based result while the TestNG window is more useful because it gives us a graphical output of the test result plus other meaningful details such as:

  - Runtimes of each method.

  - The chronological order by which methods were executed.

- TestNG is capable of generating HTML-based reports.

- Annotations can use parameters just like the usual Java methods.

Chapter 14: Introduction to Selenium Grid

What is Selenium Grid?

Selenium Grid is a part of the Selenium Suite that specializes in running multiple tests across different browsers, operating systems, and machines in parallel.

Selenium Grid has 2 versions - the older Grid 1 and the newer Grid 2. We will only focus on Grid 2 because Grid 1 is gradually being deprecated by the Selenium Team.

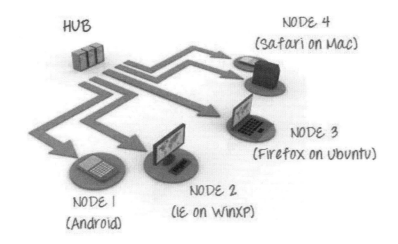

Selenium Grid uses a hub-node concept where you only run the test on a single machine called a **hub**, but the execution will be done by different machines called **nodes**.

When to Use Selenium Grid?

You should use Selenium Grid when you want to do either one or both of following:

- **Run your tests against different browsers, operating systems, and machines all at the same time.** This will ensure that the application you are **Testing** is fully compatible with a wide range of browser-O.S combinations.

- **Save time in the execution of your test suites**. If you set up Selenium Grid to run, say, 4 tests at a time, then you would be able to finish the whole suite around 4 times faster.

Grid 1.0 Vs Grid 2.0

Following are the main differences between Selenium Grid 1 and 2.

Grid 1	Grid 2
Selenium Grid 1 has its own remote control that is different from the Selenium RC server. They are two different programs.	Selenium Grid 2 is now bundled with the Selenium Server jar file
You need to install and configure **Apache** Ant first before you can use Grid 1.	You do not need to install **Apache** Ant in Grid 2.
Can only support Selenium RC commands/scripts.	Can support both Selenium RC and WebDriver scripts.
You can only automate one browser per remote control.	One remote control can automate up to 5 browsers.

Selenium Grid Architecture

The Hub

- The hub is the central point where you load your tests into.

- There should only be one hub in a grid.

- The hub is launched only on a single machine, say, a computer whose O.S is Windows 7 and whose browser is IE.

- The machine containing the hub is where the tests will be run, but you will see the browser being automated on the node.

The Nodes

- Nodes are the Selenium instances that will execute the tests that you loaded on the hub.

- There can be one or more nodes in a grid.

- Nodes can be launched on multiple machines with different platforms and browsers.

- The machines running the nodes need not be the same platform as that of the hub.

How to Set Up Selenium Grid?

In this section, you will use 2 machines. The first machine will be the system that will run the hub while the other machine will run a node. For simplicity, let us call the machine where the hub runs as "Machine A" while the machine where the node runs will be "Machine B." It is also important to note their IP addresses. Let us say that Machine A has an IP address of 192.168.1.3 while Machine B has an IP of 192.168.1.4.

Step 1

Download the Selenium Server

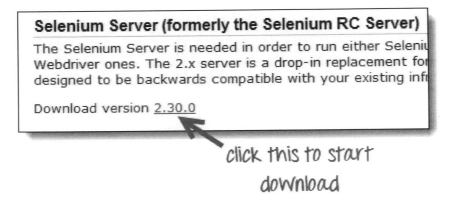

Selenium Server (formerly the Selenium RC Server)

The Selenium Server is needed in order to run either Seleni[u]
Webdriver ones. The 2.x server is a drop-in replacement fo[r]
designed to be backwards compatible with your existing infr[a]

Download version 2.30.0

click this to start download

Step 2

You can place the Selenium Server .jar file anywhere in your HardDrive. But for the purpose of this tutorial, place it on the C drive of both Machine A and Machine B. After doing this, you are now done installing Selenium Grid. The following steps will launch the hub and the node.

Step 3

- We are now going to launch a hub. Go to Machine A. Using the command prompt, navigate to the root of Machine A's - C drive, because that is the directory where we placed the Selenium Server.

- On the command prompt, type **java -jar selenium-server-standalone-2.30.0.jar -role hub**

- The hub should successfully be launched. Your command prompt should look similar to the image below

```
C:\Users\            >cd \

C:\>java -jar selenium-server-standalone-2.30.0.jar -role hub
Feb 23, 2013 4:02:11 AM org.openqa.grid.selenium.GridLauncher main
INFO: Launching a selenium grid server
2013-02-23 04:02:12.065:INFO:osjs.Server:jetty-7.x.y-SNAPSHOT
2013-02-23 04:02:12.113:INFO:osjsh.ContextHandler:started o.s.j.s.ServletContext
Handler{/,null}
2013-02-23 04:02:12.126:INFO:osjs.AbstractConnector:Started SocketConnector@0.0.
0.0:4444
Feb 23, 2013 4:02:22 AM org.openqa.grid.internal.BaseRemoteProxy <init>
WARNING: Max instance not specified. Using default = 1 instance
```

Step 4

Another way to verify whether the hub is running is by using a browser. Selenium Grid, by default, uses Machine A's port 4444 for its web interface. Simply open up a browser and go to **http://localhost:4444/grid/console**

Grid Hub 2.30.0

view config

Also, you can check if Machine B can access the hub's web interface by launching a browser there and going to where "iporhostnameofmachineA" should be the IP address or the hostname of the machine where the hub is running. Since Machine A's IP address is 192.168.1.3, then on the browser on Machine B you should type **http://192.168.1.3:4444/grid/console**

Step 5

- Now that the hub is already set up, we are going to launch a node. Go to Machine B and launch a command prompt there.

- Navigate to the root of Drive C and type the code below. We used the IP address 192.168.1.3 because that is where the hub is running. We also used port 5566 though you may choose any free port number you desire.

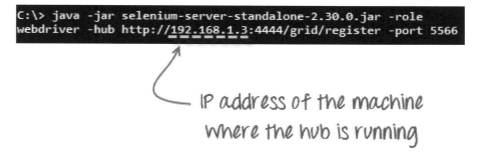

```
C:\> java -jar selenium-server-standalone-2.30.0.jar -role
webdriver -hub http://192.168.1.3:4444/grid/register -port 5566
```

IP address of the machine where the hub is running

- When you press Enter, your command prompt should be similar to the image below.

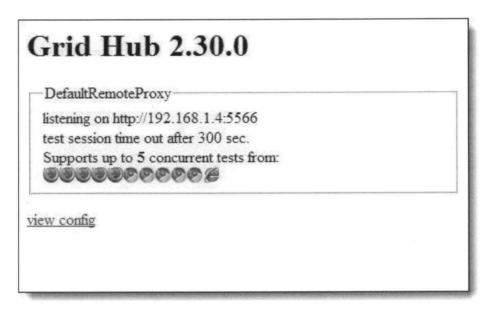

```
C:\>java -jar selenium-server-standalone-2.30.0.jar -role webdriver -hub http://
192.168.1.3:4444/grid/register -port 5566
Feb 23, 2013 4:34:39 PM org.openqa.grid.selenium.GridLauncher main
INFO: Launching a selenium grid node
16:34:40.733 INFO - Java: Oracle Corporation 23.7-b01
16:34:40.733 INFO - OS: Windows XP 5.1 x86
16:34:40.733 INFO - v2.30.0, with Core v2.30.0. Built from revision dc1ef9c
16:34:40.874 INFO - RemoteWebDriver instances should connect to: http://127.0.0.
1:5566/wd/hub
16:34:40.874 INFO - Version Jetty/5.1.x
16:34:40.874 INFO - Started HttpContext[/selenium-server/driver,/selenium-server
/driver]
16:34:40.889 INFO - Started HttpContext[/selenium-server,/selenium-server]
16:34:40.889 INFO - Started HttpContext[/,/]
16:34:40.889 INFO - Started org.openqa.jetty.jetty.servlet.ServletHandler@ed3512
16:34:40.889 INFO - Started HttpContext[/wd,/wd]
16:34:40.905 INFO - Started SocketListener on 0.0.0.0:5566
16:34:40.905 INFO - Started org.openqa.jetty.jetty.Server@1f77497
16:34:40.905 INFO - using the json request : {"class":"org.openqa.grid.common.Re
gistrationRequest","capabilities":[{"platform":"XP","seleniumProtocol":"WebDrive
r","browserName":"firefox","maxInstances":5},{"platform":"XP","seleniumProtocol"
:"WebDriver","browserName":"chrome","maxInstances":5},{"platform":"WINDOWS","sel
eniumProtocol":"WebDriver","browserName":"internet explorer","maxInstances":1}],
"configuration":{"port":5566,"register":true,"host":"192.168.1.4","proxy":"org.o
penqa.grid.selenium.proxy.DefaultRemoteProxy","maxSession":5,"role":"webdriver",
"hubHost":"192.168.1.3","registerCycle":5000,"hub":"http://192.168.1.3:4444/grid
/register","hubPort":4444,"url":"http://192.168.1.4:5566","remoteHost":"http://1
92.168.1.4:5566"}}
16:34:40.905 INFO - starting auto register thread. Will try to register every 50
00 ms.
16:34:40.905 INFO - Registering the node to hub :http://192.168.1.3:4444/grid/re
gister
16:34:46.171 INFO - Executing: org.openqa.selenium.remote.server.handler.Status@
1e5a771 at URL: /status>
16:34:46.186 INFO - Done: /status
```

Step 6

Go to the Selenium Grid web interface and refresh the page. You should see something like this.

Grid Hub 2.30.0

DefaultRemoteProxy

listening on http://192.168.1.4:5566

test session time out after 300 sec.

Supports up to 5 concurrent tests from:

view config

At this point, you have already configured a simple grid. You are now ready to run a test remotely on Machine B.

Designing Test Scripts That Can Run on the Grid

To design test scripts that will run on the grid, we need to use **DesiredCapabilites** and the **RemoteWebDriver** objects.

- **DesiredCapabilites** is used to set the type of **browser** and **OS** that we will automate

- **RemoteWebDriver** is used to set which node (or machine) that our test will run against.

To use the **DesiredCapabilites** object, you must first import this package

```
import org.openqa.selenium.remote.DesiredCapabilities;
```

To use the **RemoteWebDriver** object, you must import these packages.

```
import java.net.MalformedURLException;
import java.net.URL;
import org.openqa.selenium.remote.RemoteWebDriver;
```

Using the DesiredCapabilites Object

Go to the Grid's web interface and hover on an image of the browser that you want to automate. Take note of the **platform,** and the **browserName** showed by the tooltip.

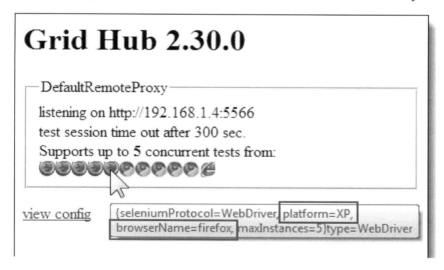

In this case, the platform is "XP" and the browserName is "Firefox."

We will use the platform and the browserName in our WebDriver as shown below (of course you need to import the necessary packages first).

```
DesiredCapabilities capability = DesiredCapabilities.firefox();
capability.setBrowserName("firefox");
capability.setPlatform(Platform.XP);
```

Using the RemoteWebDriver Object

Import the necessary packages for RemoteWebDriver and then pass the DesiredCapabilities object that we created above as a parameter for the RemoteWebDriver object.

we used RemoteWebDriver and not FirefoxDriver

```
WebDriver driver;
driver = new RemoteWebDriver(
        new URL("http://192.168.1.4:5566/wd/hub"), capability);
```

IP address and port on Machine B

Running a Sample Test Case on the Grid

Below is a simple WebDriver TestNG code that you can create in Eclipse on Machine A. Once you run it, automation will be performed on Machine B.

```java
import org.openqa.selenium.*;
import org.openqa.selenium.remote.DesiredCapabilities;
import java.net.MalformedURLException;
import java.net.URL;
import org.openqa.selenium.remote.RemoteWebDriver;
import org.testng.Assert;
import org.testng.annotations.*;

public class Grid_2 {
    WebDriver driver;
    String baseUrl, nodeURL;

    @BeforeTest
    public void setUp() throws MalformedURLException {
        baseUrl = "http://newtours.demoaut.com/";
        nodeURL = "http://192.168.1.4:5566/wd/hub";
        DesiredCapabilities capability = DesiredCapabilities.firefox();
        capability.setBrowserName("firefox");
        capability.setPlatform(Platform.XP);
        driver = new RemoteWebDriver(new URL(nodeURL), capability);
    }

    @AfterTest
    public void afterTest() {
        driver.quit();
    }

    @Test
    public void simpleTest() {
        driver.get(baseUrl);
        Assert.assertEquals("Welcome: Mercury Tours", driver.getTitle());
    }
}
```

The test should pass.

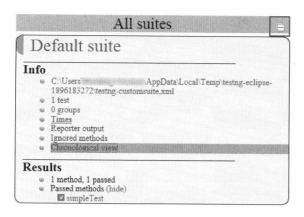

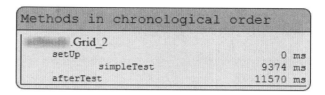

Summary

- Selenium Grid is used to run multiple tests simultaneously on different browsers and platforms.

- Grid uses the hub-node concept.

  - The hub is the central point wherein you load your tests.

  - Nodes are the Selenium instances that will execute the tests that you loaded on the hub.

- To install Selenium Grid, you only need to download the Selenium Server jar file - the same file used in running Selenium RC tests.

- There are 2 ways to verify if the hub is running: one was through the command prompt, and the other was through a browser

- To run test scripts on the Grid, you should use the DesiredCapabilities and the RemoteWebDriver objects.

  - DesiredCapabilites is used to set the type of browser and OS that we will automate

  - RemoteWebDriver is used to set which node (or machine) that our test will run against.

Chapter 15: Parameterization using XML and DataProviders: Selenium

As we create software, we always wish it should work differently with a different set of data. When it comes to **Testing** the same piece of software, we can't be unfair to test it with just one set of data. Here again, we need to verify that our system is taking all set of combinations which it expected to support.

Here comes Parameterization in the picture. To pass multiple data to the application at runtime, we need to parameterize our test scripts.

This concept which we achieve by parameterization is called **Data Driven Testing.**

Type of Parameterization in TestNG-

To make parameterization more clear, we will go through the parameterization options in one the most popular framework for Selenium Webdriver - **TestNG**.

There are **two ways** by which we can achieve parameterization in TestNG

1. With the help of **Parameters annotation** and **TestNG XML** file.

   ```
   @Parameters({"name","searchKey"})
   ```

2. With the help of **DataProvider** annotation.

   ```
   @DataProvider(name="SearchProvider")
   ```

Parameters from Testng.xml can be suite or test level

Parameter from DataProvider can take Method and ITestContext as the parameter.

Let's study them in detail -

Parameters annotation with Testng.xml

Select parameterization using annotations when you do want to deal with complexity & the number of input combinations are less.

Let see how this works

Test Scenario

Step 1) Launch browser & go to Google.com

Step 2) Enter a search keyword

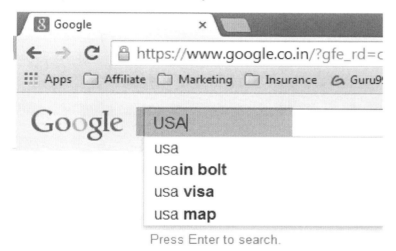

Step 3) Verify the inputted value is same as that provided by our test data

Step 4) Repeat 2 & 3 until all values are inputted

Test Author	SearchKey
Guru99	India
Krishna	USA
Bhupesh	China

Here is an example of how to do it WITHOUT parameters

```
package parameters;

import org.testng.annotations.Test;
import org.testng.AssertJUnit;
import java.util.concurrent.TimeUnit;
import org.openqa.selenium.By;
import org.openqa.selenium.WebDriver;
import org.openqa.selenium.WebElement;
import org.openqa.selenium.firefox.FirefoxDriver;

public class NoParameterWithTestNGXML {
        String driverPath = "C:\\geckodriver.exe";
        WebDriver driver;

    @Test
    public void testNoParameter() throws InterruptedException{
        String author = "guru99";
        String searchKey = "india";

        System.setProperty("webdriver.firefox.marionette", driverPath);
        driver= new FirefoxDriver();
        driver.manage().timeouts().implicitlyWait(10, TimeUnit.SECONDS);

        driver.get("https://google.com");
        WebElement searchText = driver.findElement(By.name("q"));
        //Searching text in google text box
        searchText.sendKeys(searchKey);

        System.out.println("Welcome ->"+author+" Your search key is->"+searchKey);
                System.out.println("Thread will sleep now");

        Thread.sleep(3000);
        System.out.println("Value in Google Search Box = "+searchText.getAttribute("value")
+" ::: Value given by input = "+searchKey);
        //verifying the value in google search box
        AssertJUnit.assertTrue(searchText.getAttribute("value").equalsIgnoreCase(searchKey));
}
}
```

A Study, the above example. Just imagine how complex the code will become when we do this for 3 input combinations

Now, let's parameterize this using TestNG

To do so, you will need to

- Create an XML file which will store the parameters

- In the test, add annotation @Parameters

```
@Test
@Parameters({"author","searchKey"})
public void testParameterWithXML(String author,String searchKey)
```

```
<suite name="TestSuite" thread-count="1" >
 <parameter name="author" value="demo" />
 <parameter name="searchKey" value="India" />
 <test name="testGuru">
   <classes>
     <class name="parameters.ParameterWithTestNGXML">
     </class>
   </classes>
 </test>
</suite>
```

Here 'author' parameter from xml will map with the 'author' parameter in test method

Here is the complete code

Test Level TestNG.xml

```xml
<?xml version="1.0" encoding="UTF-8"?>
<!DOCTYPE suite SYSTEM "http://testng.org/testng-1.0.dtd">
<suite name="TestSuite" thread-count="3" >
<parameter name="author" value="Guru99" />
<parameter name="searchKey" value="India" />
<test name="testGuru">
<parameter name="searchKey" value="UK" />
<classes>
<class name="parameters.ParameterWithTestNGXML">
</class>
</classes>
</test>
</suite>
```

ParameterWithTestNGXML.java File

```java
package parameters;

import org.testng.AssertJUnit;
import java.util.concurrent.TimeUnit;

import org.openqa.selenium.By;
```

```java
import org.openqa.selenium.WebDriver;
import org.openqa.selenium.WebElement;
import org.openqa.selenium.firefox.FirefoxDriver;

import org.testng.annotations.Optional;
import org.testng.annotations.Parameters;
import org.testng.annotations.Test;

public class ParameterWithTestNGXML {
        String driverPath = "C:\\geckodriver.exe";
        WebDriver driver;
    @Test
    @Parameters({"author","searchKey"})
    public void testParameterWithXML( @Optional("Abc") String author,String searchKey) throws
InterruptedException{

        System.setProperty("webdriver.firefox.marionette", driverPath);
        driver = new FirefoxDriver();
        driver.manage().timeouts().implicitlyWait(10, TimeUnit.SECONDS);
        driver.get("https://google.com");

        WebElement searchText = driver.findElement(By.name("q"));
        //Searching text in google text box
        searchText.sendKeys(searchKey);

        System.out.println("Welcome ->"+author+" Your search key is->"+searchKey);
        System.out.println("Thread will sleep now");
        Thread.sleep(3000);
        System.out.println("Value in Google Search Box = "+searchText.getAttribute("value")
+" ::: Value given by input = "+searchKey);
        //verifying the value in google search box
        AssertJUnit.assertTrue(searchText.getAttribute("value").equalsIgnoreCase(searchKey));

}
}
```

Instructions to run the script, select the XML file and Run as Test NG Suite

Right Click on .xml file -> Run as -> TestNG Suite (Note : Suite)

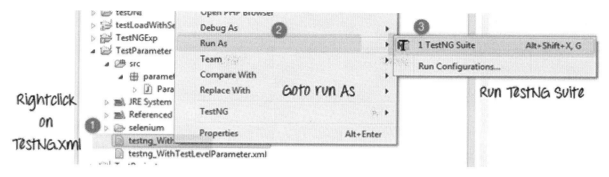

Right click on TestNGxml

Goto run As

Run TestNG suite

Now, parameters can be defined at 2 levels

1. Suite level – The parameters inside the <suite> tag of TestNG XML file will be a suite level parameter.

2. Test Level -- The parameters inside the <Test> tag of testing XML file will be a Test level parameter.

Here is the same test with suite level parameters

```xml
<?xml version="1.0" encoding="UTF-8"?>
<!DOCTYPE suite SYSTEM "http://testng.org/testng-1.0.dtd">
<suite name="TestSuite" thread-count="1" >
<parameter name="author" value="demo" />
<parameter name="searchKey" value="India" />
<test name="testGuru">
    <classes>
        <class name="parameters.ParameterWithTestNGXML">
        </class>
    </classes>
   </test>
  </suite>
```

NOTE: In case if the parameter name is same in suite level and test level then test level parameter will get preference over suite level. So, in that case, all the classes inside that test level will share the overridden parameter, and other classes which are outside the test level will share suite level parameter.

```xml
<?xml version="1.0" encoding="UTF-8"?>
<!DOCTYPE suite SYSTEM "http://testng.org/testng-1.0.dtd">
<suite name="TestTest" thread-count="1" >
 <parameter name="author" value="demo" />
 <parameter name="searchKey" value="India" />
 <test name="testGuru">
<parameter name="searchKey" value="UK" />
    <classes>
        <class name="parameters.ParameterWithTestNGXML">
        </class>
    </classes>
   </test>
  </suite>
```

Same parameter in suite and test level

Troubleshooting

ISSUE # 1 Parameter value in testng.xml cannot be typecasted to the corresponding test method's parameter it will throw an error.

Consider the following example

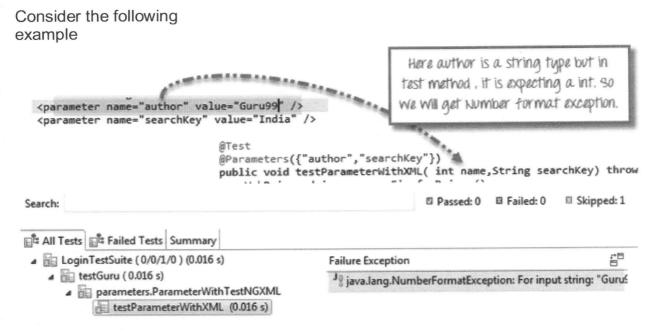

Here, 'author' attribute is equal to 'Guru99' which is a string and in corresponding test method its expecting an integer value, so we will get an exception here.

ISSUE # 2 Your @Parameters do not have a corresponding value in testing.xml.

You can solve this situation by adding **@optional annotation** in the corresponding parameter in the test method.

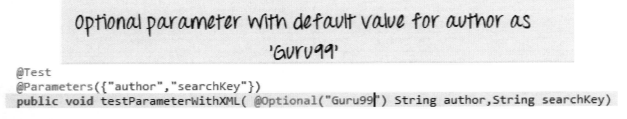

ISSUE # 3: You want to test multiple values of the same parameter using Testng.xml

The Simple answer is this can not be done! You can have multiple different parameters, but each parameter can only have a single value. This helps prevent hardcoding values into the script. This makes code reusable. Think of it as config files for your script. If you want to use multiple values for a parameter use DataProviders

Parameters using Dataprovider

@Parameters annotation is easy but to test with multiple sets of data we need to use Data Provider.

To fill thousand's of web forms using our testing framework we need a different methodology which can give us a very large dataset in a single execution flow.

This data driven concept is achieved by **@DataProvider** annotation in TestNG.

```
@DataProvider(name="SearchProvider")
public Object[][] getDataFromDataprovider(){
```

It has only one **attribute 'name'**. If you do not specify the name attribute then the DataProvider's name will be same as the corresponding method name.

Data provider returns **a two-dimensional JAVA object** to the test method and the test method, will invoke M times in a M*N type of object array. For example, if the DataProvider returns an array of 2*3 objects, the corresponding testcase will be invoked 2 times with 3 parameters each time.

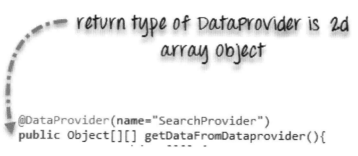

```
@DataProvider(name="SearchProvider")
public Object[][] getDataFromDataprovider(){
```

Complete Example

```
package parameters;


import java.util.concurrent.TimeUnit;
```

```java
import org.openqa.selenium.By;
import org.openqa.selenium.WebDriver;
import org.openqa.selenium.WebElement;
import org.openqa.selenium.firefox.FirefoxDriver;

import org.testng.Assert;
import org.testng.annotations.BeforeTest;
import org.testng.annotations.DataProvider;
import org.testng.annotations.Test;

public class ParameterByDataprovider {
    WebDriver driver;
    String driverPath = "C:\\geckodriver.exe";

    @BeforeTest
    public void setup(){
        //Create firefox driver object
        System.setProperty("webdriver.firefox.marionette", driverPath);
        driver = new FirefoxDriver();
        driver.manage().timeouts().implicitlyWait(10, TimeUnit.SECONDS);
        driver.get("https://google.com");
    }

    /** Test case to verify google search box
     * @param author
     * @param searchKey
     * @throws InterruptedException
     */

    @Test(dataProvider="SearchProvider")
    public void testMethod(String author,String searchKey) throws InterruptedException{
    {
        WebElement searchText = driver.findElement(By.name("q"));
        //search value in google searchbox
        searchText.sendKeys(searchKey);
        System.out.println("Welcome ->"+author+" Your search key is->"+searchKey);
        Thread.sleep(3000);
        String testValue = searchText.getAttribute("value");
        System.out.println(testValue +":::::"+searchKey);
        searchText.clear();
        //Verify if the value in google search box is correct
        Assert.assertTrue(testValue.equalsIgnoreCase(searchKey));
    }
    }
```

```
/**
 * @return Object[][] where first column contains 'author'
 * and second column contains 'searchKey'
 */

@DataProvider(name="SearchProvider")
public Object[][] getDataFromDataprovider(){
return new Object[][]
    {
        { "Guru99", "India" },
        { "Krishna", "UK" },
        { "Bhupesh", "USA" }
    };

}

}
```

Invoke DataProvider from different class

By default, DataProvider resides in the same class where test method is or its base class. To put it in some other class we need to make data provider method as static and in test method we need to add an attribute **dataProviderClass** in **@Test** annotation.

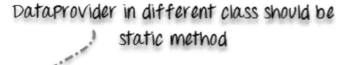

```
ublic class DataproviderClass {
    @DataProvider(name="SearchProvider")
    public  static Object[][]  getDataFromDataprovider(){
        return new Object[][] {
            { "Mr. A", "India" },
```

Code Example

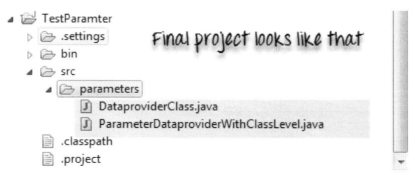

TestClass ParameterDataproviderWithClassLevel.java

```java
package parameters;

import java.util.concurrent.TimeUnit;
import org.openqa.selenium.By;
import org.openqa.selenium.WebDriver;
import org.openqa.selenium.WebElement;
import org.openqa.selenium.firefox.FirefoxDriver;
import org.testng.Assert;
import org.testng.annotations.BeforeTest;
import org.testng.annotations.Test;

public class ParameterDataproviderWithClassLevel {
    WebDriver driver;
    String driverPath = "C:\\geckodriver.exe";

        @BeforeTest
    public void setup(){
                System.setProperty("webdriver.firefox.marionette", driverPath);
                driver = new FirefoxDriver();
        driver.manage().timeouts().implicitlyWait(10, TimeUnit.SECONDS);
        driver.get("https://google.com");
    }

    @Test(dataProvider="SearchProvider",dataProviderClass=DataproviderClass.class)
    public void testMethod(String author,String searchKey) throws InterruptedException{

        WebElement searchText = driver.findElement(By.name("q"));
        //Search text in google text box
        searchText.sendKeys(searchKey);
        System.out.println("Welcome ->"+author+" Your search key is->"+searchKey);
        Thread.sleep(3000);
        //get text from search box
        String testValue = searchText.getAttribute("value");
        System.out.println(testValue +":::::"+searchKey);
        searchText.clear();
        //verify if search box has correct value
        Assert.assertTrue(testValue.equalsIgnoreCase(searchKey));
    }
}
```

DataproviderClass.java

```java
package parameters;

import org.testng.annotations.DataProvider;
public class DataproviderClass {
        @DataProvider(name="SearchProvider")
```

```
        public static Object[][] getDataFromDataprovider(){
            return new Object[][] {
                { "Guru99", "India" },
                { "Krishna", "UK" },
                { "Bhupesh", "USA" }
            };
}}
```

Types of Parameters in Dataprovider

There are two type of parameters supported by DataProvider method.

Method- If the **SAME** DataProvider should behave differently with different test method , use Method parameter.

```
@DataProvider(name="SearchProvider")
public Object[][] getDataFromDataprovider(Method m){
    if(m.getName().equalsIgnoreCase("testMethodA")){
    return new Object[][] {
            { "Guru99", "India" },
            { "Krishna", "UK" },
            { "Bhupesh", "USA" }
        };}
    else{
        return new Object[][] {
                { "Canada" },
                { "Russia" },
                { "Japan" }
            };
    }

}
```

Method parameter in data provider

In the following example ,

- We check if method name is testMethodA.
- If yes return one set of value
- Else return another set of value

```
package parameters;

import java.lang.reflect.Method;
import java.util.concurrent.TimeUnit;
import org.openqa.selenium.By;
import org.openqa.selenium.WebDriver;
import org.openqa.selenium.WebElement;
import org.openqa.selenium.firefox.FirefoxDriver;
import org.testng.Assert;
import org.testng.annotations.BeforeTest;
import org.testng.annotations.DataProvider;
```

```java
import org.testng.annotations.Test;

public class ParameterByMethodInDataprovider{

    WebDriver driver;
    String driverPath = "C:\\geckodriver.exe";

    @BeforeTest
    public void setup(){
        System.setProperty("webdriver.firefox.marionette", driverPath);
        driver = new FirefoxDriver();
        driver.manage().timeouts().implicitlyWait(10, TimeUnit.SECONDS);
        driver.get("https://google.com");
    }

    @Test(dataProvider="SearchProvider")
    public void testMethodA(String author,String searchKey) throws InterruptedException{

        WebElement searchText = driver.findElement(By.name("q"));
        //Search text in search box
        searchText.sendKeys(searchKey);
        //Print author and search string
        System.out.println("Welcome ->"+author+" Your search key is->"+searchKey);
        Thread.sleep(3000);
        String testValue = searchText.getAttribute("value");
        System.out.println(testValue +":::"+searchKey);
        searchText.clear();
        //Verify if google text box is showing correct value
        Assert.assertTrue(testValue.equalsIgnoreCase(searchKey));
    }

    @Test(dataProvider="SearchProvider")
    public void testMethodB(String searchKey) throws InterruptedException{
        {
        WebElement searchText = driver.findElement(By.name("q"));
            //Search text in search box
            searchText.sendKeys(searchKey);
            //Print only search string
            System.out.println("Welcome ->Unknown user Your search key is->"+searchKey);
            Thread.sleep(3000);
            String testValue = searchText.getAttribute("value");
            System.out.println(testValue +":::"+searchKey);
            searchText.clear();
            //Verify if google text box is showing correct value
            Assert.assertTrue(testValue.equalsIgnoreCase(searchKey));
```

```
        }
    }
    /**
     * Here DataProvider returning value on the basis of test method name
     * @param m
     * @return
     **/


    @DataProvider(name="SearchProvider")
    public Object[][] getDataFromDataprovider(Method m){
        if(m.getName().equalsIgnoreCase("testMethodA")){
        return new Object[][] {
                { "Guru99", "India" },
                { "Krishna", "UK" },
                { "Bhupesh", "USA" }
            };}
        else{
        return new Object[][] {
                { "Canada" },
                { "Russia" },
                { "Japan" }
            };}
    }
}
```

Here is the output

```
Welcome ->Guru99 Your search key is->India
India::::India
Welcome ->Krishna Your search key is->UK
UK::::UK
Welcome ->Bhupesh Your search key is->USA
USA::::USA
Welcome ->Unknown user Your search key is->Canada
Canada::::Canada
Welcome ->Unknown user Your search key is->Russia
Russia::::Russia
Welcome ->Unknown user Your search key is->Japan
Japan::::Japan
PASSED: testMethodA("Guru99", "India")
PASSED: testMethodA("Krishna", "UK")
PASSED: testMethodA("Bhupesh", "USA")
PASSED: testMethodB("Canada")
PASSED: testMethodB("Russia")            Output
PASSED: testMethodB("Japan")


===============================================
    Default test
    Tests run: 6, Failures: 0, Skips: 0
===============================================
```

ITestContext- It can use to create different parameters for test cases based on groups.

In real-life, you can use ITestContext to vary parameter values based on Test Methods, hosts, configurations of the test.

```java
@DataProvider(name="SearchProvider")
public Object[][] getDataFromDataprovider(ITestContext c){
Object[][] groupArray = null;
    for (String group : c.getIncludedGroups()) {
    if(group.equalsIgnoreCase("A")){
        groupArray = new Object[][] {
                    { "Guru99", "India" },
                    { "Krishna", "UK" },
                    { "Bhupesh", "USA" }
            };
    break;
    }
        else if(group.equalsIgnoreCase("B"))
        {
        groupArray = new Object[][] {
                    { "Canada" },
                    { "Russia" },
                    { "Japan" }
            };
        }
    break;
    }

    return groupArray;
    }
}
```

ITestContext Paramter in Data provider

In the following code example

- We have 2 groups A & B

- Each test method is assigned to a group

- If value of group is A, a particular data set is returned

- If value of group is B, another data set is returned

```java
package parameters;

import java.util.concurrent.TimeUnit;
import org.openqa.selenium.By;
import org.openqa.selenium.WebDriver;
import org.openqa.selenium.WebElement;
import org.openqa.selenium.firefox.FirefoxDriver;
import org.testng.Assert;
import org.testng.ITestContext;
import org.testng.annotations.BeforeTest;
import org.testng.annotations.DataProvider;
import org.testng.annotations.Test;

public class ParameterByITestContextInDataprovider {
        WebDriver driver;
```

```java
        String driverPath = "C:\\geckodriver.exe";
        @BeforeTest(groups={"A","B"})
        public void setup(){
                System.setProperty("webdriver.firefox.marionette", driverPath);
                        driver = new FirefoxDriver();
                        driver.manage().timeouts().implicitlyWait(10, TimeUnit.SECONDS);
                        driver.get("https://google.com");

        }


        @Test(dataProvider="SearchProvider",groups="A")
        public void testMethodA(String author,String searchKey) throws InterruptedException{
                {
                  //search google textbox
                        WebElement searchText = driver.findElement(By.name("q"));
                        //search a value on it
                        searchText.sendKeys(searchKey);
                        System.out.println("Welcome ->"+author+" Your search key is-
>"+searchKey);

                        Thread.sleep(3000);
                        String testValue = searchText.getAttribute("value");
                        System.out.println(testValue +"::::"+searchKey);
                        searchText.clear();
                        //verify correct value in searchbox
                        Assert.assertTrue(testValue.equalsIgnoreCase(searchKey));
        }
        }

        @Test(dataProvider="SearchProvider",groups="B")
        public void testMethodB(String searchKey) throws InterruptedException{
                {
                  //find google search box
                        WebElement searchText = driver.findElement(By.name("q"));
                        //search a value on it
                        searchText.sendKeys(searchKey);
                        System.out.println("Welcome ->Unknown user Your search key is-
>"+searchKey);

                        Thread.sleep(3000);
                        String testValue = searchText.getAttribute("value");
                        System.out.println(testValue +"::::"+searchKey);
                        searchText.clear();
                        //verify correct value in searchbox
                        Assert.assertTrue(testValue.equalsIgnoreCase(searchKey));
        }
        }
```

```
    /**
     * Here the DAtaProvider will provide Object array on the basis on ITestContext
     * @param c
     * @return
     */
    @DataProvider(name="SearchProvider")
    public Object[][] getDataFromDataprovider(ITestContext c){
    Object[][] groupArray = null;
            for (String group : c.getIncludedGroups()) {
            if(group.equalsIgnoreCase("A")){
                    groupArray = new Object[][] {
                                    { "Guru99", "India" },
                                    { "Krishna", "UK" },
                                    { "Bhupesh", "USA" }
                            };
            break;
            }
                    else if(group.equalsIgnoreCase("B"))
                    {
                    groupArray = new Object[][] {
                                        { "Canada" },
                                        { "Russia" },
                                        { "Japan" }
                                    };
                    }
            break;
        }
        return groupArray;
        }
}
```

Summary:

- **Parameterization** is require to create **Data Driven Testing**.

- TestNG support two kinds of parameterization, using **@Parameter+TestNG.xml** and using **@DataProvider**

- In **@Parameter+TestNG.xml** parameters can be placed in suite level and test level. If

  The Same parameter name is declared in both places; test level parameter will get preference over suit level parameter.

- using @Parameter+TestNG.xml only one value can be set at a time, but @DataProvider return **an 2d array of Object**.

- If DataProvider is present in the different class then the class where the test method resides, **DataProvider** should be **static method**.

- There are two parameters supported by **DataProvider** are **Method** and **ITestContext.**

Chapter 16: Cross Browser Testing using Selenium

What is Cross Browser Testing?

Cross Browser Testing is a type of functional test to check that your web application works as expected in different browsers.

Why do we need Cross Browser Testing?

Web-based applications are totally different from Windows applications. A web application can be opened in any browser by the end user. For example, some people prefer to open **http://twitter.com** in**Firefox browser**, while other's can be using **Chrome browser** or **IE**.

In the diagram below you can observe that in **IE**, the login box of Twitter is not showing curve at all corners, but we are able to see it in Chrome browser.

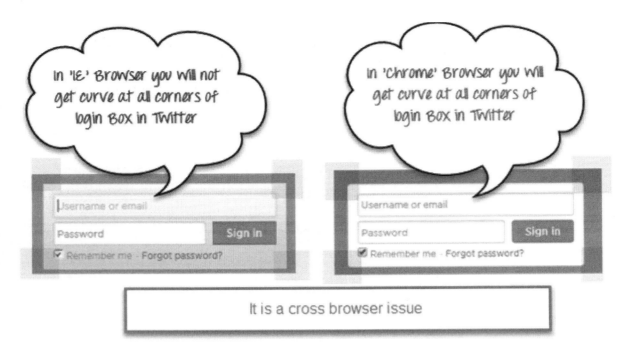

So we need to ensure that the web application will work as expected in all popular browsers so that more people can access it and use it.

This motive can be fulfilled with Cross Browser **Testing** of the product.

Reason Cross Browser Issues

1. Font size mismatch in different browsers.

2. JavaScript implementation can be different.

3. CSS,HTML validation difference can be there.

4. Some browser still not supporting HTML5.

5. Page alignment and div size.

6. Image orientation.

7. Browser incompatibility with OS. Etc.

How to perform Cross Browser Testing

If we are using Selenium WebDriver, we can automate test cases using Internet Explorer, FireFox, Chrome, Safari browsers.

To execute test cases with different browsers in the same machine at the same time we can integrate TestNG framework with Selenium WebDriver.

Your testing.xml will look like that,

```xml
<?xml version="1.0" encoding="UTF-8"?>
<!DOCTYPE suite SYSTEM "http://testng.org/testng-1.0.dtd">
<suite name="TestSuite" thread-count="2" parallel="tests" >
  <test name="ChromeTest">
  <parameter name="browser" value="Chrome" />
    <classes>
       <class name="parallelTest.CrossBrowserScript">
       </class>
    </classes>
  </test>
  <test name="FirefoxTest">
  <parameter name="browser" value="Firefox" />
    <classes>
       <class name="parallelTest.CrossBrowserScript">
       </class>
    </classes>
  </test>
</suite>
```

Test will run parallel

1st Test name is 'ChromeTest'

Parameter is 'Chrome'

2st Test name is 'FirefoxTest'

Parameter is 'Firefox'

This is the TestNG.xml for cross Browser Testing

This testing.xml will map with the test case which will look like that

Parameter will be pass from testNG.xml

```java
@BeforeTest
@Parameters("browser")
public void setup(String browser) throws Exception{
    if(browser.equalsIgnoreCase("firefox")){
    driver = new FirefoxDriver();
    }
    else if(browser.equalsIgnoreCase("chrome")){
        System.setProperty("webdriver.chrome.driver",".\\chromedriver.exe");
        driver = new ChromeDriver();
    }
}
```

check parameter value and create WebDriver according it

Here because the testing.xml has two Test tags ('ChromeTest','FirefoxTest'),this test case will execute two times for 2 different browsers.

First Test 'ChromeTest' will pass the value of parameter 'browser' as 'chrome' so ChromeDriver will be executed. This test case will run on Chrome browser.

Second Test 'FirefoxTest' will pass the value of parameter 'browser' as 'Firefox' so FirefoxDriver will be executed. This test case will run on FireFox browser.

Complete Code:

Guru99CrossBrowserScript.java

```java
package parallelTest;

import java.util.concurrent.TimeUnit;
import org.openqa.selenium.By;
import org.openqa.selenium.WebDriver;
```

```java
import org.openqa.selenium.WebElement;
import org.openqa.selenium.chrome.ChromeDriver;
import org.openqa.selenium.edge.EdgeDriver;
import org.openqa.selenium.firefox.FirefoxDriver;
import org.testng.annotations.BeforeTest;
import org.testng.annotations.Parameters;
import org.testng.annotations.Test;

public class CrossBrowserScript {

        WebDriver driver;

        /**
         * This function will execute before each Test tag in testng.xml
         * @param browser
         * @throws Exception
         */
        @BeforeTest
        @Parameters("browser")
        public void setup(String browser) throws Exception{
                //Check if parameter passed from TestNG is 'firefox'
                if(browser.equalsIgnoreCase("firefox")){
                //create firefox instance
                        System.setProperty("webdriver.firefox.marionette",
".\\geckodriver.exe");

                        driver = new FirefoxDriver();
                }
                //Check if parameter passed as 'chrome'
                else if(browser.equalsIgnoreCase("chrome")){
                        //set path to chromedriver.exe
                        System.setProperty("webdriver.chrome.driver",".\\chromedriver.exe");
                        //create chrome instance
                        driver = new ChromeDriver();
                }
                //Check if parameter passed as 'Edge'
                                else if(browser.equalsIgnoreCase("Edge")){
                                        //set path to Edge.exe

        System.setProperty("webdriver.edge.driver",".\\MicrosoftWebDriver.exe");
                                        //create Edge instance
                                        driver = new EdgeDriver();
                                }
                else{
                        //If no browser passed throw exception
                        throw new Exception("Browser is not correct");
```

```java
                }
                driver.manage().timeouts().implicitlyWait(10, TimeUnit.SECONDS);
        }

        @Test
        public void testParameterWithXML() throws InterruptedException{
                driver.get("http://demo.guru99.com/V4/");
                //Find user name
                WebElement userName = driver.findElement(By.name("uid"));
                //Fill user name
                userName.sendKeys("guru99");
                //Find password
                WebElement password = driver.findElement(By.name("password"));
                //Fill password
                password.sendKeys("guru99");
        }
}
```

testing.xml

```xml
<?xml version="1.0" encoding="UTF-8"?>

<!DOCTYPE suite SYSTEM "http://testng.org/testng-1.0.dtd">

<suite name="TestSuite" thread-count="2" parallel="tests" >

<test name="ChromeTest">

<parameter name="browser" value="Chrome" />

<classes>

<class name="parallelTest.CrossBrowserScript">

</class>

</classes>

</test>

<test name="FirefoxTest">

<parameter name="browser" value="Firefox" />

<classes>

<class name="parallelTest.CrossBrowserScript">
```

```
</class>

</classes>

</test>

<test name="EdgeTest">

<parameter name="browser" value="Edge" />

<classes>

<class name="parallelTest.CrossBrowserScript">

</class>

</classes>

</test>

</suite>
```

NOTE: To run the test, Right click on the **testing.xml,** Select Run As, and Click TestNG

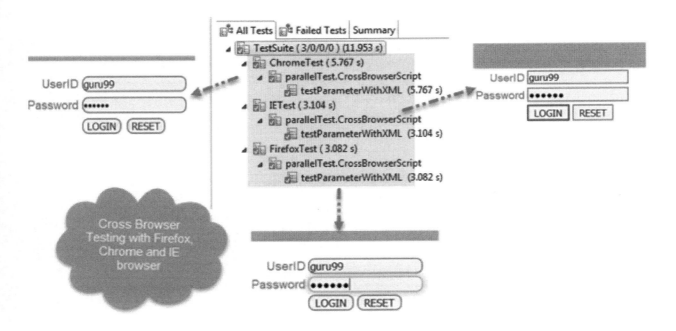

Summary

1. Cross browser Testing is a technique to test web application with different web browsers.

2. Selenium can support different type of browsers for automation.

3. Selenium can be integrated with TestNG to perform Multi Browser Testing.

4. From parameters in testing.xml we can pass browser name, and in a test case, we can create WebDriver reference accordingly.

Note: The given program was built & tested on selenium 3.0.1, Chrome 56.0.2924.87 , Firefox 47.0.2 & Microsoft Edge 14.14393. If the programs give an error, please update the driver

Chapter 17: All About Excel in Selenium: POI & JXL

File IO is a critical part of any software process. We frequently create a file, open it & update something or delete it in our Computers. Same is the case with Selenium Automation. We need a process to manipulate files with Selenium.

Java provides us different classes for File Manipulation with Selenium. In this tutorial, we are going to learn how can we read and write on **Excel** file with the help of **Java** IO package and **Apache** POI library.

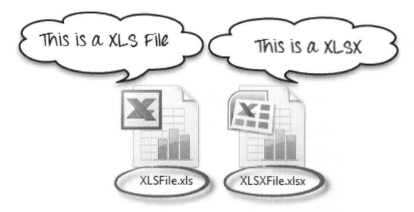

Exporting Excel

• **How to handle excel file using POI (Maven POM Dependency)**

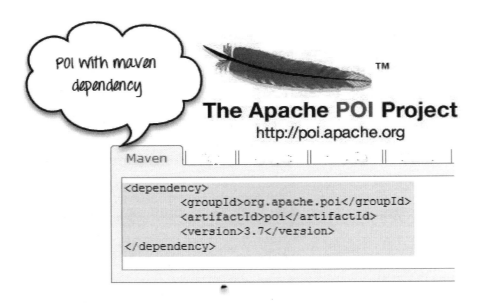

To read or write an Excel,Apache provides a very famous library POI. This library is capable enough to read and write both **XLS** and **XLSX** file format of Excel.

To read **XLS** files, an **HSSF** implementation is provided by POI library.

To read **XLSX, XSSF** implementation of **POI library** will be the choice. Let's study these implementations in detail.

If you are using Maven in your project, the Maven dependency will be

<dependency>

<groupId>org.apache.poi</groupId>

<artifactId>poi</artifactId>

<version>3.9</version>

</dependency>

Or you can simply download the latest version POI jars from **http://poi.apache.org/download.html** & download **poi-bin-3.10-FINAL-20140208.zip**

The Apache POI Project
http://poi.apache.org

Apache | POI

- **Overview**
  - Home
  - Download
  - Components
  - Text Extraction
  - Encryption support
  - Case Studies
  - Legal
- **Help**
  - Javadocs
  - FAQ
  - Mailing Lists
  - Bug Database
  - Changes Log
- **Getting Involved**
  - Subversion Repository
  - How To Build
  - Contribution Guidelines
  - Who We Are
- **Component API**
  - Excel
  - Word
  - Power
  - Open
  - OLE2
  - OLE2 D
    (HPSF)
  - Outlook (HSMF)
  - Visio (HDGF)
  - TNEF (HMEF)
  - Publisher (HPBF)
- **Apache Wide**
  - Apache Software

Apache PO

Available Downloads

This page provides instructions on how to download and verify the Apache POI
see the project homepage.

- The latest stable release is Apache POI 3.10-FINAL
- Archives of all prior releases

Apache POI releases are available under the Apache License, Version 2.0. See

To insure that you have downloaded the true release you should verify the inte

8 February 2014 - POI 3.10-FINAL available

The Apache POI team is pleased to announce the release of 3.10-FINAL. This in

A full list of changes is available in the change log. People interested should als

The POI source release as well as the pre-built binary deployment packages are
"org.apache.poi" and Version "3.10-FINAL".

Binary Distribution

- poi-bin-3.10-FINAL-20140208.tar.gz (16MB, signed)
  MD5 checksum: 818d1e99a2efe539ba49f622b554950c
  SHA1 checksum: 28b61005d780e00604fb8053fd46ab1b9b18392f
- poi-bin-3.10-FINAL-20140208.zip (23MB, signed)
  MD5 checksum: c304bc0a3163697d31e029f63450a962
  SHA1 checksum: 704f103bca893e3d4df5c2cc95d275b0cd5d0b33

> Download this

When you download the zip file for this jar, you need to unzip it and add these all jars to the
class path of your project.

docs	6/30/2014 5:01 PM	File folder	
lib	6/30/2014 5:01 PM	File folder	
ooxml-lib	6/30/2014 5:00 PM	File folder	
LICENSE	1/16/2014 10:07 AM	File	27 KB
NOTICE	1/16/2014 10:07 AM	File	1 KB
poi-3.10-FINAL-20140208.jar	2/1/2014 7:30 PM	Executable Jar File	1,906 KB
poi-examples-3.10-FINAL-20140208.jar	2/1/2014 7:30 PM	Executable Jar File	306 KB
poi-excelant-3.10-FINAL-20140208.jar	2/1/2014 7:30 PM	Executable Jar File	30 KB
poi-ooxml-3.10-FINAL-20140208.jar	2/1/2014 7:30 PM	Executable Jar File	1,008 KB
poi-ooxml-schemas-3.10-FINAL-20140208.jar	2/1/2014 7:30 PM	Executable Jar File	4,831 KB
poi-scratchpad-3.10-FINAL-20140208.jar	2/1/2014 7:30 PM	Executable Jar File	1,212 KB

ooxml folder

dom4j-1.6.1.jar	1/16/2014 10:12 AM	Executable Jar File	307 KB
stax-api-1.0.1.jar	1/16/2014 10:13 AM	Executable Jar File	26 KB
xmlbeans-2.3.0.jar	1/16/2014 10:13 AM	Executable Jar File	2,605 KB

lib folder

commons-codec-1.5.jar	1/16/2014 10:12 AM	Executable Jar File	72 KB
commons-logging-1.1.jar	1/16/2014 10:12 AM	Executable Jar File	52 KB
junit-4.11.jar	1/16/2014 10:12 AM	Executable Jar File	240 KB
log4j-1.2.13.jar	1/16/2014 10:12 AM	Executable Jar File	350 KB

Add all these Files

Classes and Interfaces in POI:

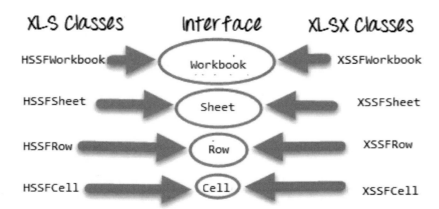

Following is a list of different Java Interfaces and classes in **POI** for reading **XLS** and **XLSX** file-

- **Workbook**: XSSFWorkbook and HSSFWorkbook classes implement this interface.

- **XSSFWorkbook**: Is a class representation of XLSX file.

- **HSSFWorkbook**: Is a class representation of XLS file.

- **Sheet**: XSSFSheet and HSSFSheet classes implement this interface.

- **XSSFSheet**: Is a class representing a sheet in an XLSX file.

- **HSSFSheet**: Is a class representing a sheet in an XLS file.

- **Row**: XSSFRow and HSSFRow classes implement this interface.

- **XSSFRow**: Is a class representing a row in the sheet of XLSX file.

- **HSSFRow**: Is a class representing a row in the sheet of XLS file.

- **Cell**: XSSFCell and HSSFCell classes implement this interface.

- **XSSFCell**: Is a class representing a cell in a row of XLSX file.

- **HSSFCell:** Is a class representing a cell in a row of XLS file.

Read/Write operation-

For our example, we will consider below given Excel file format

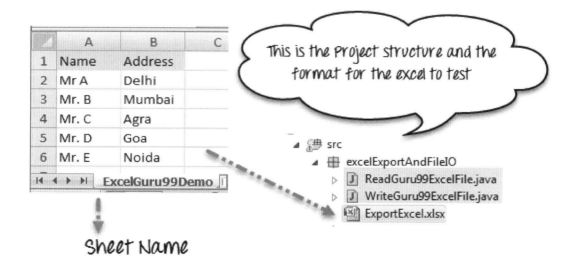

Read data from Excel file

Complete Example: Here we are trying to read data from Excel file

```
package excelExportAndFileIO;

import java.io.File;

import java.io.FileInputStream;

import java.io.IOException;
```

```java
import org.apache.poi.hssf.usermodel.HSSFWorkbook;

import org.apache.poi.ss.usermodel.Row;

import org.apache.poi.ss.usermodel.Sheet;

import org.apache.poi.ss.usermodel.Workbook;

import org.apache.poi.xssf.usermodel.XSSFWorkbook;

public class ReadGuru99ExcelFile {


    public void readExcel(String filePath,String fileName,String sheetName) throws
IOException{

    //Create an object of File class to open xlsx file

    File file =    new File(filePath+"\\"+fileName);

    //Create an object of FileInputStream class to read excel file

    FileInputStream inputStream = new FileInputStream(file);

    Workbook guru99Workbook = null;

    //Find the file extension by splitting file name in substring  and getting only extension
name

    String fileExtensionName = fileName.substring(fileName.indexOf("."));

    //Check condition if the file is xlsx file

    if(fileExtensionName.equals(".xlsx")){

    //If it is xlsx file then create object of XSSFWorkbook class

    guru99Workbook = new XSSFWorkbook(inputStream);

    }

    //Check condition if the file is xls file

    else if(fileExtensionName.equals(".xls")){
```

```java
    //If it is xls file then create object of XSSFWorkbook class

    guru99Workbook = new HSSFWorkbook(inputStream);

}

//Read sheet inside the workbook by its name

Sheet guru99Sheet = guru99Workbook.getSheet(sheetName);

//Find number of rows in excel file

int rowCount = guru99Sheet.getLastRowNum()-guru99Sheet.getFirstRowNum();

//Create a loop over all the rows of excel file to read it

for (int i = 0; i < rowCount+1; i++) {

    Row row = guru99Sheet.getRow(i);

    //Create a loop to print cell values in a row

    for (int j = 0; j < row.getLastCellNum(); j++) {

        //Print Excel data in console

        System.out.print(row.getCell(j).getStringCellValue()+"|| ");

    }

    System.out.println();

}



}



//Main function is calling readExcel function to read data from excel file

public static void main(String...strings) throws IOException{
```

```
//Create an object of ReadGuru99ExcelFile class

ReadGuru99ExcelFile objExcelFile = new ReadGuru99ExcelFile();

//Prepare the path of excel file

String filePath = System.getProperty("user.dir")+"\\src\\excelExportAndFileIO";

//Call read file method of the class to read data

objExcelFile.readExcel(filePath,"ExportExcel.xlsx","ExcelGuru99Demo");

    }

}
```

Note: We are not using the TestNG framework here. Run the class as Java Application

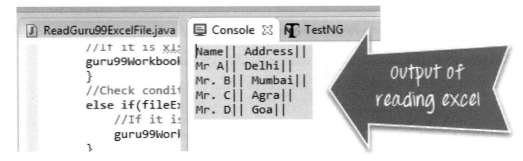

Write data on Excel file

Complete Example: Here we are trying to write data from Excel file by adding new row in Excel file

```
package excelExportAndFileIO;

import java.io.File;

import java.io.FileInputStream;

import java.io.FileOutputStream;

import java.io.IOException;

import org.apache.poi.hssf.usermodel.HSSFWorkbook;
```

```java
import org.apache.poi.ss.usermodel.Cell;

import org.apache.poi.ss.usermodel.Row;

import org.apache.poi.ss.usermodel.Sheet;

import org.apache.poi.ss.usermodel.Workbook;

import org.apache.poi.xssf.usermodel.XSSFWorkbook;

public class WriteGuru99ExcelFile {


    public void writeExcel(String filePath,String fileName,String sheetName,String[]
dataToWrite) throws IOException{

        //Create an object of File class to open xlsx file

        File file =    new File(filePath+"\\"+fileName);

        //Create an object of FileInputStream class to read excel file

        FileInputStream inputStream = new FileInputStream(file);

        Workbook guru99Workbook = null;

        //Find the file extension by splitting  file name in substring and getting only
extension name

        String fileExtensionName = fileName.substring(fileName.indexOf("."));

        //Check condition if the file is xlsx file

        if(fileExtensionName.equals(".xlsx")){

        //If it is xlsx file then create object of XSSFWorkbook class

        guru99Workbook = new XSSFWorkbook(inputStream);

        }

        //Check condition if the file is xls file

        else if(fileExtensionName.equals(".xls")){
```

```java
        //If it is xls file then create object of XSSFWorkbook class

        guru99Workbook = new HSSFWorkbook(inputStream);

    }


//Read excel sheet by sheet name

Sheet sheet = guru99Workbook.getSheet(sheetName);

//Get the current count of rows in excel file

int rowCount = sheet.getLastRowNum()-sheet.getFirstRowNum();

//Get the first row from the sheet

Row row = sheet.getRow(0);

//Create a new row and append it at last of sheet

Row newRow = sheet.createRow(rowCount+1);

//Create a loop over the cell of newly created Row

for(int j = 0; j < row.getLastCellNum(); j++){

    //Fill data in row

    Cell cell = newRow.createCell(j);

    cell.setCellValue(dataToWrite[j]);

}

//Close input stream

inputStream.close();

//Create an object of FileOutputStream class to create write data in excel file

FileOutputStream outputStream = new FileOutputStream(file);
```

```java
        //write data in the excel file

        guru99Workbook.write(outputStream);

        //close output stream

        outputStream.close();


    }



    public static void main(String...strings) throws IOException{

        //Create an array with the data in the same order in which you expect to be filled in
excel file

        String[] valueToWrite = {"Mr. E","Noida"};

        //Create an object of current class

        WriteGuru99ExcelFile objExcelFile = new WriteGuru99ExcelFile();

        //Write the file using file name, sheet name and the data to be filled


objExcelFile.writeExcel(System.getProperty("user.dir")+"\\src\\excelExportAndFileIO","ExportE
xcel.xlsx","ExcelGuru99Demo",valueToWrite);


    }

}

}
```

After Writing Excel File

```java
public static void main(String...strings) throws
    //Create an array with the data in the same c
    String[] valueToWrite = {"Mr. E","Noida"};
    //Create an object of current class
    WriteGuru99ExcelFile objExcelFile = new Write
    //Write the file using file name , sheet name
    objExcelFile.writeExcel(System.getProperty("
}
```

1	Name	Address
2	Mr A	Delhi
3	Mr. B	Mumbai
4	Mr. C	Agra
5	Mr. D	Goa
6	Mr. E	Noida

◄ ◄ ► ►│ ExcelGuru99Demo

Ready   100%

New Entry in excel file(name='Mr E' ,Address='Noida')

Excel Manipulation using JXL API

JXL A Java Excel API - A Java API to read, write, and modify Excel

JXL is also another famous jar for reading writing Excel files. Now a day's POI is used in most of the projects, but before POI, JXL was only Java API for Excel manipulation. It is a very small and simple API.

TIPS: MY SUGGESTION IS NOT TO USE JXL IN ANY NEW PROJECT BECAUSE THE LIBRARY IS NOT IN ACTIVE DEVELOPMENT FROM 2010 AND LACK OF THE FEATURE IN COMPARE TO POI API.

Download JXL:

If you want to work with JXL, you can download it from this link

http://sourceforge.net/projects/jexcelapi/files/jexcelapi/2.6.12/

Click on this link to download JXL

Home / jexcelapi / 2.6.12

Name ⬍	Modified ⬍	Size ⬍	Downloads / Week ⬍		
⬆ Parent folder					
2_6_12_releasenotes.txt	2009-10-26	606 Bytes	66		❶
jexcelapi_2_6_12.zip	2009-10-26	2.5 MB	1,030		❶
jexcelapi_2_6_12.tar.gz	2009-10-26	1.9 MB	70		❶
Totals: 3 Items		4.4 MB	1,166		

You can also get demo example inside this zipped file for JXL.

Some of the features:

- JXL is able to read Excel 95, 97, 2000, XP, 2003 workbook.
- We can work with English, French, Spanish, German.
- Copying a Chart and image insertion in Excel is possible

Drawback:

- We can write Excel 97 and later only (writing in Excel 95 is not supported).

- JXL does not support XLSX format of excel file.
- It Generates spreadsheet in Excel 2000 format.

Summary:

- Excel file can be read by Java IO operation. For that, we need to use **Apache POI Jar**.
- There are two kinds of a workbook in Excel file, **XLSX** and **XLS** files.
- POI has different Interfaces Workbook, Sheet, Row, Cell.
- These interfaces are implemented by corresponding **XLS** (**HSSFWorkbook, HSSFSheet, HSSFRow, HSSFCell**) and **XLSX** (**XSSFWorkbook, XSSFSheet, XSSFRow, XSSFCell**) file manipulation classes.
- JXL is another API for Excel manipulation.
- JXL cannot work with XLSX format of excel.

Chapter 18: Creating Keyword & Hybrid Frameworks with Selenium

What is Selenium Framework?

Selenium Framework is a code structure that helps to make code maintenance easy. Without frameworks, we will place the "code" as well as "data" in the same place which is neither re-usable nor readable. Using Frameworks, produce beneficial outcomes like increased code re-usage, higher portability, reduced script maintenance cost, higher code readability, etc.

There are mainly three type of frameworks created by Selenium WebDriver to automate manual test cases

- Data Driven Test Framework
- Keyword Driven Test Framework
- Hybrid Test Framework

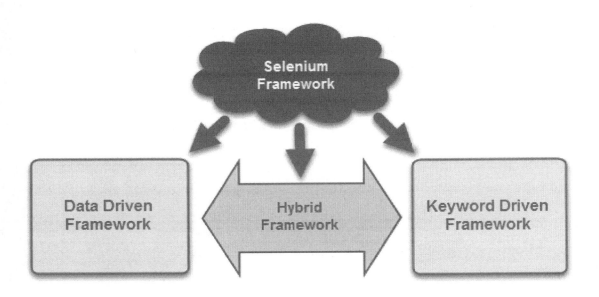

Data Driven Test Framework

In data driven framework all of our test data is generated from some external files like **Excel**, CSV, XML or some database table. We already learned about Data Driven **Testing** in our previous **tutorial**

Keyword Driven Test Framework:

In keyword driven test framework, all the operations and instructions are written in some external file like Excel worksheet. Here is how the complete framework looks like

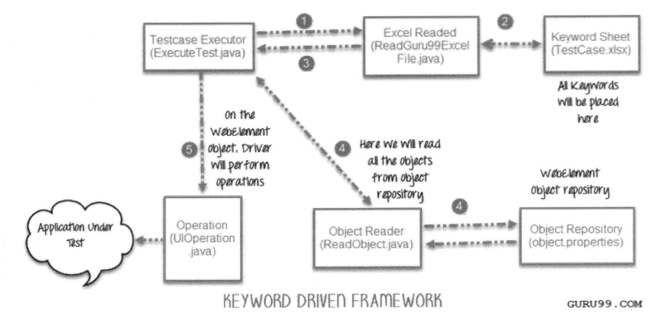

As you can see it's a 5 step framework. Let's study it stepwise in detail

Step 1)

- The driver script Execute.java will call ReadGuru99ExcelFile.java

- ReadGuru99ExcelFile.java has POI script to read data from an Excel

Step 2)

- ReadGuru99ExcelFile.java will read data from TestCase.xlsx

- Here is how the sheet looks like-

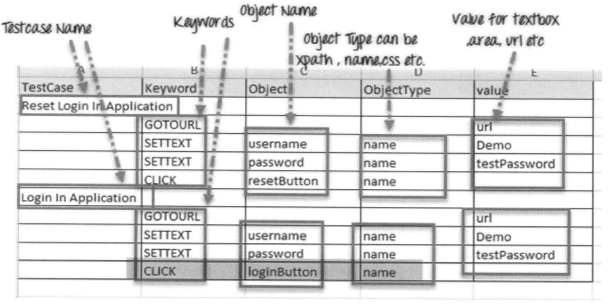

Excel Sheet For Keyword Driven Test

- According to the keywords written in Excel file, the framework will perform the operation on UI.

- For example, we need to click a button 'Login.' Correspondingly, our Excel will have a keyword 'Click.' Now the AUT can have hundreds of button on a page, to identify a Login button, in Excel we will input Object Name as loginButton & object type as a name (see highlighted the row in above image). The Object Type could be Xpath, name CSS or any other value

Step 3) ReadGuru99ExcelFile.java will pass this data to the driver script Execute.java

Step 4)

- For all of our UI web elements, we need to create an object repository where we will place their element locator (like Xpath, name, CSS path, class name etc.)

This will be our object repository

- Execute.java (our driver script) will read the entire Object Repository and store it in a variable

- To read this object repository, we need a ReadObject class which has a getObjectRepository method to read it.

```java
public class ReadObject {

    Properties p = new Properties();

    public Properties getObjectRepository() throws
        //Read object repository file
        InputStream stream = new FileInputStream(ne
        //load all objects
        p.load(stream);
        return p;
    }
}
```

This class will be used to read object repository file

NOTE: You may think why do we need to create an object repository. The answer helps in code maintenance. For example, we are using the button with name = btnlogin in 10 different test cases. In future, the developer decides to change the name from btnlogin to submit. You will have to make a change in all the 10 test cases. In the case of an object repository, you will make the change just once in the repository.

Step 5)

- The driver will pass the data from Excel & Object Repository to UIOperation class

- UIOperation class has functions to perform actions corresponding to keywords like CLICK, SETTEXT etc… mentioned in the excel

- UIOperation class is a **Java** class which has the actual implementation of the code to perform operations on web elements

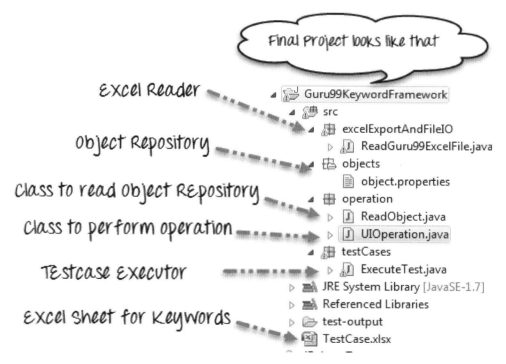

function to execute keywords

Keyword File

TestCase	Keyword	Object
Reset Login In Application		
	GOTOURL	
	SETTEXT	usernar
	SETTEXT	passwo
	CLICK	resetBu¬g c
Login in Application		

```java
public void perform(Properties
    System.out.println("");
    switch (operation.toUpperCase
    case "CLICK":
        driver.findElement(this.getObject(p,objectName,objectType)).click();
        break;
    case "SETTEXT":
        driver.findElement(this.getObject(p,objectName,objectType)).sendKeys
        break;

    case "GOTOURL":
        driver.get(p.getProperty(value));
        break;
    case "GETTEXT":
        driver.findElement(this.getObject(p,objectName,objectType)).getText(
        break;
```

The complete project will look like-

Final Project looks like that

- **Excel Reader** → Guru99KeywordFramework
  - src
    - **excelExportAndFileIO**
      - ReadGuru99ExcelFile.java
    - **Object Repository** → objects
      - object.properties
    - operation
      - **Class to read Object Repository** → ReadObject.java
      - **Class to perform operation** → UIOperation.java
    - testCases
      - **Testcase Executor** → ExecuteTest.java
  - JRE System Library [JavaSE-1.7]
  - Referenced Libraries
  - test-output
  - **Excel Sheet for Keywords** → TestCase.xlsx

Let's look into an example:

Test Scenario

- We are executing 2 test cases
- Test Case 1:

- Goto **http://demo.guru99.com/V4/**

- Enter User ID

- Enter Password

- Click Reset

- Test Case 2:

- Goto **http://demo.guru99.com/V4/**

- Enter User ID

- Enter Password

- Click Login

object.properties

url=**http://demo.guru99.com/V4/**

username=uid

password=password

title=barone

loginButton=btnLogin

resetButton=btnReset

ReadGuru99ExcelFile.java

```java
package excelExportAndFileIO;
import java.io.File;
import java.io.FileInputStream;
import java.io.IOException;
import org.apache.poi.hssf.usermodel.HSSFWorkbook;
import org.apache.poi.ss.usermodel.Sheet;
import org.apache.poi.ss.usermodel.Workbook;
import org.apache.poi.xssf.usermodel.XSSFWorkbook;
public class ReadGuru99ExcelFile {

    public Sheet readExcel(String filePath,String fileName,String sheetName) throws
IOException{
    //Create a object of File class to open xlsx file
    File file =    new File(filePath+"\\"+fileName);
```

```java
//Create an object of FileInputStream class to read excel file
    FileInputStream inputStream = new FileInputStream(file);
    Workbook guru99Workbook = null;
    //Find the file extension by spliting file name in substing and getting only extension
name
    String fileExtensionName = fileName.substring(fileName.indexOf("."));
    //Check condition if the file is xlsx file
    if(fileExtensionName.equals(".xlsx")){
    //If it is xlsx file then create object of XSSFWorkbook class
    guru99Workbook = new XSSFWorkbook(inputStream);
    }
    //Check condition if the file is xls file
    else if(fileExtensionName.equals(".xls")){
        //If it is xls file then create object of XSSFWorkbook class
        guru99Workbook = new HSSFWorkbook(inputStream);
    }
    //Read sheet inside the workbook by its name
    Sheet guru99Sheet = guru99Workbook.getSheet(sheetName);
     return guru99Sheet;
    }
}
```

ReadObject.java

```java
package operation;
import java.io.File;
import java.io.FileInputStream;
import java.io.IOException;
import java.io.InputStream;
import java.util.Properties;
public class ReadObject {
    Properties p = new Properties();
    public Properties getObjectRepository() throws IOException{
        //Read object repository file
        InputStream stream = new FileInputStream(new
File(System.getProperty("user.dir")+"\\src\\objects\\object.properties"));
        //load all objects
        p.load(stream);
         return p;
    }

}
```

UIOperation.java

```java
package operation;
import java.util.Properties;
import org.openqa.selenium.By;
import org.openqa.selenium.WebDriver;
public class UIOperation {
    WebDriver driver;
    public UIOperation(WebDriver driver){
        this.driver = driver;
    }
    public void perform(Properties p,String operation,String objectName,String
objectType,String value) throws Exception{
        System.out.println("");
        switch (operation.toUpperCase()) {
        case "CLICK":
            //Perform click
            driver.findElement(this.getObject(p,objectName,objectType)).click();
            break;
        case "SETTEXT":
            //Set text on control
            driver.findElement(this.getObject(p,objectName,objectType)).sendKeys(value);
            break;

        case "GOTOURL":
            //Get url of application
            driver.get(p.getProperty(value));
            break;
        case "GETTEXT":
            //Get text of an element
            driver.findElement(this.getObject(p,objectName,objectType)).getText();
            break;
        default:
            break;
        }
    }

    /**
     * Find element BY using object type and value
     * @param p
     * @param objectName
     * @param objectType
     * @return
     * @throws Exception
     */
```

```java
private By getObject(Properties p,String objectName,String objectType) throws Exception{
    //Find by xpath
    if(objectType.equalsIgnoreCase("XPATH")){

        return By.xpath(p.getProperty(objectName));
    }
    //find by class
    else if(objectType.equalsIgnoreCase("CLASSNAME")){

        return By.className(p.getProperty(objectName));

    }
    //find by name
    else if(objectType.equalsIgnoreCase("NAME")){

        return By.name(p.getProperty(objectName));

    }
    //Find by css
    else if(objectType.equalsIgnoreCase("CSS")){

        return By.cssSelector(p.getProperty(objectName));

    }
    //find by link
    else if(objectType.equalsIgnoreCase("LINK")){

        return By.linkText(p.getProperty(objectName));

    }
    //find by partial link
    else if(objectType.equalsIgnoreCase("PARTIALLINK")){

        return By.partialLinkText(p.getProperty(objectName));

    }else
    {
        throw new Exception("Wrong object type");
    }
}
}
```

ExecuteTest.java

```java
package testCases;
import java.util.Properties;
import operation.ReadObject;
import operation.UIOperation;
import org.apache.poi.ss.usermodel.Row;
import org.apache.poi.ss.usermodel.Sheet;
import org.openqa.selenium.WebDriver;
import org.openqa.selenium.firefox.FirefoxDriver;
import org.testng.annotations.Test;
import excelExportAndFileIO.ReadGuru99ExcelFile;
public class ExecuteTest {
@Test
    public void testLogin() throws Exception {
        // TODO Auto-generated method stub
WebDriver webdriver = new FirefoxDriver();
ReadGuru99ExcelFile file = new ReadGuru99ExcelFile();
ReadObject object = new ReadObject();
Properties allObjects = object.getObjectRepository();
UIOperation operation = new UIOperation(webdriver);
//Read keyword sheet
Sheet guru99Sheet = file.readExcel(System.getProperty("user.dir")+"\\","TestCase.xlsx" ,
"KeywordFramework");
//Find number of rows in excel file
    int rowCount = guru99Sheet.getLastRowNum()-guru99Sheet.getFirstRowNum();
    //Create a loop over all the rows of excel file to read it
    for (int i = 1; i < rowCount+1; i++) {
        //Loop over all the rows
        Row row = guru99Sheet.getRow(i);
        //Check if the first cell contain a value, if yes, That means it is the new testcase
name
        if(row.getCell(0).toString().length()==0){
        //Print testcase detail on console
            System.out.println(row.getCell(1).toString()+"----"+ row.getCell(2).toString()+"-
---"+
            row.getCell(3).toString()+"----"+ row.getCell(4).toString());
        //Call perform function to perform operation on UI
            operation.perform(allObjects, row.getCell(1).toString(),
row.getCell(2).toString(),
                row.getCell(3).toString(), row.getCell(4).toString());
    }
        else{
            //Print the new testcase name when it started
                System.out.println("New Testcase->"+row.getCell(0).toString() +" Started");
```

```
            }
         }
      }
}
```

After execution, output will look like -

```
New Testcase->Reset Login In Application Started
GOTOURL------------url

SETTEXT----username----name----Demo

SETTEXT----password----name----testPassword

CLICK----resetButton----name----

New Testcase->Login In Application Started
GOTOURL------------url

SETTEXT----username----name----Demo

SETTEXT----password----name----testPassword

CLICK----loginButton----name----

PASSED: testLogin
```

Two Test cases

Hybrid Test Framework

Hybrid Test framework is a concept where we are using the advantage of both Keyword and Data driven framework.

Here for keywords, we will use Excel files to maintain test cases, and for test data, we can use data, provider of TestNG framework.

```
@DataProvider(name="hybridData")
public Object[][] getDataFromDataprovider() thr
    Object[][] object = null;
    ReadGuru99ExcelFile file = new ReadGuru99Ex

    //Read keyword sheet
    ...

@Test(dataProvider="hybridData")
public void testLogin(String testcaseName,String keywo
    // TODO Auto-generated method stub

    if(testcaseName!=null&&testcaseName.length()!=0){
    webdriver=new FirefoxDriver();
    }
    ReadObject object = new ReadObject();
    Properties allObjects =  object.getObjectRepositor
    UIOperation operation = new UIOperation(webdriver)
    //Call perform function to perform operation on UI
            operation.perform(allObjects, keyword, obj
                 objectType, value);
```

This test case is same as keyword driven , but we also have a dataprovider

Here in our hybrid framework, we don't need to change anything in Keyword driven framework, here we just need to replace ExecuteTest.java file with HybridExecuteTest.java file.

only Testcase is changed in hybrid test case , all other thing will work without any changes

This HybridExecuteTest file has all the code for keyword driven with data provider concept.

The complete pictorial representation of hybrid framework will look like

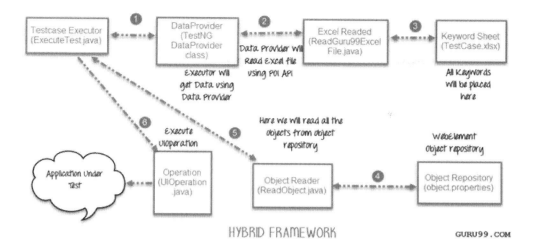

HYBRID FRAMEWORK   GURU99.COM

HybridExecuteTest.java

```java
package testCases;
import java.io.IOException;
import java.util.Properties;
import operation.ReadObject;
import operation.UIOperation;
import org.apache.poi.ss.usermodel.Row;
import org.apache.poi.ss.usermodel.Sheet;
import org.openqa.selenium.WebDriver;
import org.openqa.selenium.firefox.FirefoxDriver;
import org.testng.annotations.DataProvider;
import org.testng.annotations.Test;
import excelExportAndFileIO.ReadGuru99ExcelFile;
public class HybridExecuteTest {
    WebDriver webdriver = null;
@Test(dataProvider="hybridData")
    public void testLogin(String testcaseName,String keyword,String objectName,String
objectType,String value) throws Exception {
        // TODO Auto-generated method stub

    if(testcaseName!=null&&testcaseName.length()!=0){
    webdriver=new FirefoxDriver();
    }
ReadObject object = new ReadObject();
Properties allObjects = object.getObjectRepository();
UIOperation operation = new UIOperation(webdriver);
    //Call perform function to perform operation on UI
            operation.perform(allObjects, keyword, objectName,
                objectType, value);
```

```java
        }
@DataProvider(name="hybridData")
    public Object[][] getDataFromDataprovider() throws IOException{
    Object[][] object = null;
    ReadGuru99ExcelFile file = new ReadGuru99ExcelFile();
//Read keyword sheet
Sheet guru99Sheet = file.readExcel(System.getProperty("user.dir")+"\\","TestCase.xlsx" ,
"KeywordFramework");
//Find number of rows in excel file
    int rowCount = guru99Sheet.getLastRowNum()-guru99Sheet.getFirstRowNum();
    object = new Object[rowCount][5];
    for (int i = 0; i < rowCount; i++) {
        //Loop over all the rows
        Row row = guru99Sheet.getRow(i+1);
        //Create a loop to print cell values in a row
        for (int j = 0; j < row.getLastCellNum(); j++) {
            //Print excel data in console
            object[i][j] = row.getCell(j).toString();
        }
    }
    System.out.println("");
     return object;
    }
}
```

Summary:

- We can create three types of test framework using Selenium WebDriver.

- These are Data Driven, Keyword Driven, and Hybrid test framework.

- We can achieve Data-driven framework using TestNG's data provider.

- In Keyword driven framework, keywords are written in some external files like excel file and java code will call this file and execute test cases.

- The hybrid framework is a mix of keyword driven and data driven framework.

Chapter 19: Page Object Model (POM) & Page Factory in Selenium: Ultimate Guide

Before we learn about Page Object Model, let's understand -

Why POM?

Starting an UI Automation in Selenium WebDriver is NOT a tough task. You just need to find elements, perform operations on it.

Consider this simple script to login into a website

```
public class NoPOMTest99GuruLogin {

    /**
     * This test case will login in http://demo.guru99.com/V4/
     * Verify login page title as guru99 bank
     * Login to application
     * Verify the home page using Dashboard message
     */
    @Test(priority=0)
    public void test_Home_Page_Appear_Correct(){
        WebDriver driver = new FirefoxDriver();
        driver.manage().timeouts().implicitlyWait(10, TimeUnit.SECONDS);
        driver.get("http://demo.guru99.com/V4/");
        //Find user name and fill user name          ❶ Find user name and fill it
        driver.findElement(By.name("uid")).sendKeys("demo");
        //find password and fill it                   ❷ Find password and fill it
        driver.findElement(By.name("password")).sendKeys("password");
        //click login button                          ❸ Find home
        driver.findElement(By.name("btnLogin")).click();  Find Login button and click it  page text
        String homeText = driver.findElement(By.xpath("//table//tr[@class='heading3']")).getText();  ❹ and get it
        //verify login success
        Assert.assertTrue(homeText.toLowerCase().contains("guru99 bank"));
    }
                            ❺ Verify home page has text 'Guru99 Bank'
}
```

As you can observe, all we are doing is finding elements and filling values for those elements.

This is a small script. Script maintenance looks easy. But with time test suite will grow. As you add more and more lines to your code, things become tough.

The chief problem with script maintenance is that if 10 different scripts are using the same page element, with any change in that element, you need to change all 10 scripts. This is time consuming and error prone.

A better approach to script maintenance is to create a separate class file which would find web elements, fill them or verify them. This class can be reused in all the scripts using that element. In future, if there is a change in the web element, we need to make the change in just 1 class file and not 10 different scripts.

This approach is called **Page Object Model(POM)**. It helps make the code **more readable, maintainable**, and **reusable**.

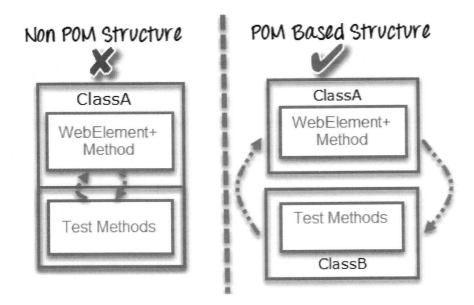

What is POM?

- **Page Object Model** is a design pattern to create **Object Repository** for web UI elements.

- Under this model, for each web page in the application, there should be corresponding page class.

- This Page class will find the WebElements of that web page and also contains Page methods which perform operations on those WebElements.

- Name of these methods should be given as per the task they are performing, i.e., if a loader is waiting for the payment gateway to appear, POM method name can be waitForPaymentScreenDisplay().

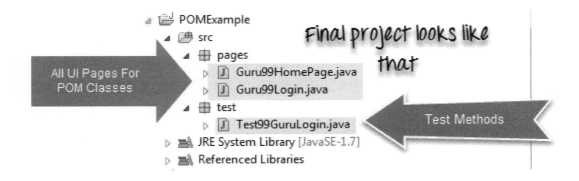

Advantages of POM

1. Page Object Patten says operations and flows in the UI should be separated from verification. This concept makes our code cleaner and easy to understand.

2. The Second benefit is the **object repository is independent of test cases**, so we can use the same object repository for a different purpose with different tools. For example, we can integrate POM with TestNG/JUnit for functional **Testing** and at the same time with JBehave/Cucumber for acceptance testing.

3. Code becomes less and optimized because of the reusable page methods in the POM classes.

4. **Methods** get **more realistic names** which can be easily mapped with the operation happening in UI. i.e. if after clicking on the button we land on the home page, the method name will be like 'gotoHomePage()'.

How to implement POM?

Simple POM:

It's the basic structure of Page object model (POM) where all Web Elements of the **AUT** and the method that operate on these Web Elements are maintained inside a class file.A task like **verification** should be **separate** as part of Test methods.

```
public class Guru99Login {        ← Page class in object repository  ❶

    WebDriver driver;
    By user99GuruName = By.name("uid");
    By password99Guru = By.name("password");
    By titleText =By.className("barone");        Find Web Element
    By login = By.name("btnLogin");

    public Guru99Login(WebDriver driver){        Performing operation on web
        this.driver = driver;                                      element
    }
    //Set user name in textbox
    public void setUserName(String strUserName){
        driver.findElement(user99GuruName).sendKeys(strUserName);  ❸
    }                          ❷
}
```

Complete Example

TestCase: Go to Guru99 Demo Site.

Step 1) Go to Guru99 Demo Site

Goto Guru99 Demo site

demo.guru99.com/V4/

Step 2) In home page check text **"Guru99 Bank"** is present

Verify if you found this title 'Guru99 Bank' in Login Page

Guru99 Bank

Step 3) Login into application

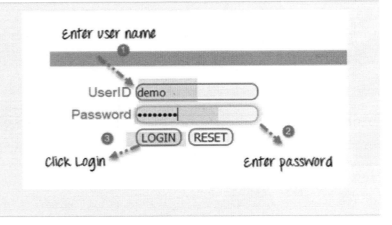

Enter user name

① UserID demo

Password ••••••••

③ LOGIN RESET ②

Click Login   Enter password

Step 4) Verify that the Home page contains text as "Manger Id: demo"

Welcome To Manager's Page of Guru99 Bank

Manger Id : demo

User Name should appear on Home Page

Here are we are dealing with 2 pages

1. Login Page

2. Home Page (shown once you login)

Accordingly, we create 2 POM classes

Guru99 Login page POM

```java
package pages;

import org.openqa.selenium.By;

import org.openqa.selenium.WebDriver;

public class Guru99Login {

    WebDriver driver;

    By user99GuruName = By.name("uid");

    By password99Guru = By.name("password");

    By titleText =By.className("barone");

    By login = By.name("btnLogin");


    public Guru99Login(WebDriver driver){

        this.driver = driver;

    }

    //Set user name in textbox

    public void setUserName(String strUserName){

        driver.findElement(user99GuruName).sendKeys(strUserName);;

    }



    //Set password in password textbox

    public void setPassword(String strPassword){

        driver.findElement(password99Guru).sendKeys(strPassword);

    }
```

```java
//Click on login button

public void clickLogin(){

        driver.findElement(login).click();

}


//Get the title of Login Page

public String getLoginTitle(){

 return     driver.findElement(titleText).getText();

}

/**

 * This POM method will be exposed in test case to login in the application

 * @param strUserName

 * @param strPasword

 * @return

 */

public void loginToGuru99(String strUserName,String strPasword){

    //Fill user name

    this.setUserName(strUserName);

    //Fill password

    this.setPassword(strPasword);

    //Click Login button

    this.clickLogin();
```

```
    }

}
```

Guru99 Home Page POM

```java
package pages;

import org.openqa.selenium.By;

import org.openqa.selenium.WebDriver;

public class Guru99HomePage {

    WebDriver driver;

    By homePageUserName = By.xpath("//table//tr[@class='heading3']");


    public Guru99HomePage(WebDriver driver){

        this.driver = driver;

    }



    //Get the User name from Home Page

        public String getHomePageDashboardUserName(){

         return    driver.findElement(homePageUserName).getText();

        }

}
```

Guru99 Simple POM Test case

```java
package test;

import java.util.concurrent.TimeUnit;

import org.openqa.selenium.WebDriver;
```

```java
import org.openqa.selenium.firefox.FirefoxDriver;

import org.testng.Assert;

import org.testng.annotations.BeforeTest;

import org.testng.annotations.Test;

import pages.Guru99HomePage;

import pages.Guru99Login;

public class Test99GuruLogin {

    WebDriver driver;

    Guru99Login objLogin;

    Guru99HomePage objHomePage;


    @BeforeTest

    public void setup(){

        driver = new FirefoxDriver();

        driver.manage().timeouts().implicitlyWait(10, TimeUnit.SECONDS);

        driver.get("http://demo.guru99.com/V4/");

    }

    /**

     * This test case will login in http://demo.guru99.com/V4/

     * Verify login page title as guru99 bank

     * Login to application

     * Verify the home page using Dashboard message
```

```
    */

    @Test(priority=0)

    public void test_Home_Page_Appear_Correct(){

        //Create Login Page object

    objLogin = new Guru99Login(driver);

    //Verify login page title

    String loginPageTitle = objLogin.getLoginTitle();

    Assert.assertTrue(loginPageTitle.toLowerCase().contains("guru99 bank"));

    //login to application

    objLogin.loginToGuru99("mgr123", "mgr!23");

    // go the next page

    objHomePage = new Guru99HomePage(driver);

    //Verify home page


Assert.assertTrue(objHomePage.getHomePageDashboardUserName().toLowerCase().contains("manger
id : mgr123"));

    }
```

What is Page Factory?

Page Factory is an inbuilt Page Object Model concept for Selenium WebDriver but it is very optimized.

Here as well, we follow the concept of separation of Page Object Repository and Test Methods. Additionally, with the help of PageFactory class, we use annotations **@FindBy** to find WebElement. We use initElements method to initialize web elements

static initElements method of
PageFactory class for
initializing webElement

```
@FindBy(xpath="//table//tr[@class='heading3']")
WebElement homePageUserName;

public Guru99HomePage(WebDriver driver){
    this.driver = driver;
    //This initElements method will create  all WebElements
    PageFactory.initElements(driver, this);
}
```

@FindBy can accept **tagName, partialLinkText, name, linkText, id, css, className, xpath** as attributes.

Let's look at the same example as above using Page Factory

Guru99 Login page with Page Factory

```java
package PageFactory;

import org.openqa.selenium.WebDriver;

import org.openqa.selenium.WebElement;

import org.openqa.selenium.support.FindBy;

import org.openqa.selenium.support.PageFactory;

public class Guru99Login {

    /**

     * All WebElements are identified by @FindBy annotation

     */

    WebDriver driver;

    @FindBy(name="uid")

    WebElement user99GuruName;
```

```java
@FindBy(name="password")

WebElement password99Guru;


@FindBy(className="barone")

WebElement titleText;


@FindBy(name="btnLogin")

WebElement login;


public Guru99Login(WebDriver driver){

    this.driver = driver;

    //This initElements method will create all WebElements

    PageFactory.initElements(driver, this);

}

//Set user name in textbox

public void setUserName(String strUserName){

    user99GuruName.sendKeys(strUserName);



}



//Set password in password textbox

public void setPassword(String strPassword){

password99Guru.sendKeys(strPassword);
```

```java
}


//Click on login button

public void clickLogin(){

        login.click();

}


//Get the title of Login Page

public String getLoginTitle(){

 return    titleText.getText();

}
/**

 * This POM method will be exposed in test case to login in the application

 * @param strUserName

 * @param strPasword

 * @return

 */

public void loginToGuru99(String strUserName,String strPasword){

    //Fill user name

    this.setUserName(strUserName);

    //Fill password

    this.setPassword(strPasword);
```

```
                    //Click Login button

        this.clickLogin();


    }

}
```

Guru99 Home Page with Page Factory

```
package PageFactory;

import org.openqa.selenium.WebDriver;

import org.openqa.selenium.WebElement;

import org.openqa.selenium.support.FindBy;

import org.openqa.selenium.support.PageFactory;

public class Guru99HomePage {

    WebDriver driver;

    @FindBy(xpath="//table//tr[@class='heading3']")

    WebElement homePageUserName;


    public Guru99HomePage(WebDriver driver){

        this.driver = driver;

        //This initElements method will create all WebElements

        PageFactory.initElements(driver, this);

    }


    //Get the User name from Home Page

        public String getHomePageDashboardUserName(){
```

```
        return    homePageUserName.getText();

    }

}
```

Guru99 TestCase with Page Factory concept

```
package test;

import java.util.concurrent.TimeUnit;

import org.openqa.selenium.WebDriver;

import org.openqa.selenium.firefox.FirefoxDriver;

import org.testng.Assert;

import org.testng.annotations.BeforeTest;

import org.testng.annotations.Test;

import PageFactory.Guru99HomePage;

import PageFactory.Guru99Login;

public class Test99GuruLoginWithPageFactory {

    WebDriver driver;

    Guru99Login objLogin;

    Guru99HomePage objHomePage;


    @BeforeTest

    public void setup(){

        driver = new FirefoxDriver();
```

```java
        driver.manage().timeouts().implicitlyWait(10, TimeUnit.SECONDS);

        driver.get("http://demo.guru99.com/V4/");

}

/**

 * This test go to http://demo.guru99.com/V4/

 * Verify login page title as guru99 bank

 * Login to application

 * Verify the home page using Dashboard message

 */

@Test(priority=0)

public void test_Home_Page_Appear_Correct(){

    //Create Login Page object

objLogin = new Guru99Login(driver);

//Verify login page title

String loginPageTitle = objLogin.getLoginTitle();

Assert.assertTrue(loginPageTitle.toLowerCase().contains("guru99 bank"));

//login to application

objLogin.loginToGuru99("mgr123", "mgr!23");

// go the next page

objHomePage = new Guru99HomePage(driver);

//Verify home page
```

```
Assert.assertTrue(objHomePage.getHomePageDashboardUserName().toLowerCase().contains("manger
id : mgr123"));


    }



}
```
Complete Project Structure will look like the diagram:

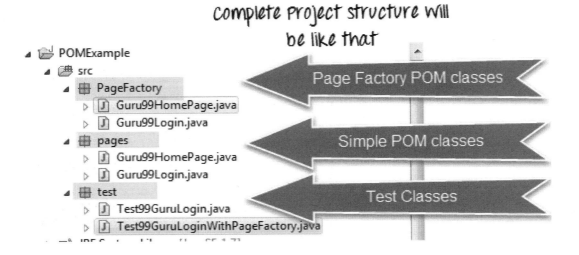

AjaxElementLocatorFactory

One of the key advantages of using Page Factory pattern is AjaxElementLocatorFactory Class.

It is working on lazy loading concept, i.e. a timeout for a WebElement will be assigned to the Object page class with the help of AjaxElementLocatorFactory .

Here, when an operation is performed on an element the wait for its visibility starts from that moment only. If the element is not found in the given time interval, test case execution will throw 'NoSuchElementException' exception.

after 100 sec if element is not visible to perform an operation, timeout exception will appear

```
AjaxElementLocatorFactory factory = new AjaxElementLocatorFactory(driver, 100);
PageFactory.initElements(factory, this);
```

This is a lazy loading,wait will start only if we perform operation on control

Summary

1. Page Object Model is an Object Repository design pattern in Selenium WebDriver.

2. POM creates our testing code maintainable, reusable.

3. Page Factory is an optimized way to create object repository in POM concept.

4. AjaxElementLocatorFactory is a lazy load concept in Page Factory pattern to identify WebElements only when they are used in any operation.

Chapter 20: PDF, Emails and Screenshot of Test Reports in Selenium

Before we look into anything else, let's first understand -

Why do we need reporting?

When we are using Selenium or any other automation tool, we are performing operations on the web application. But our purpose of automation is not just to exercise the Application Under Test. We, as an automation tester are supposed to test the application, find bugs and report it to the development team or higher management. Here the reporting gets importance for software **Testing** process

TestNG Reporting

TestNG library provides a very handy reporting feature. After execution, TestNG will generate a test-output folder at the root of the project. This folder contains two type of Reports-

Index.html: This is the complete report of current execution which contains information like an error, groups, time, reporter logs, testng XML files.

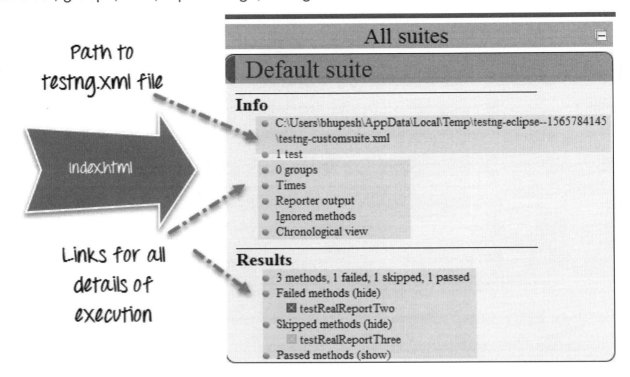

emailable-report.html: This is the summarize report of the current test execution which contains test case message in green (for pass test cases) and red(for failed test cases) highlight.

Test	# Passed	# Skipped	# Failed	Time (ms)	Included Groups
Default suite					
Default test	1	1	1	37	

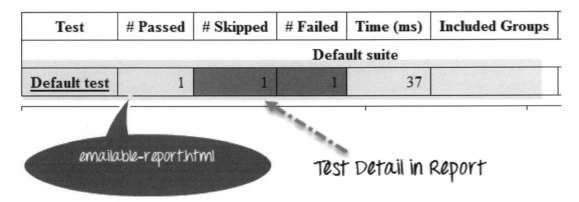

How to customize TestNG Report

TestNG reporting is quite handy but still, sometimes we need some less data in reports or want to display reports in some other format like pdf, excel, etc. or want to change report's layout.

There can be two ways we can customize TestNG report

- Using ITestListener Interface:
- Using IReporter Interface:

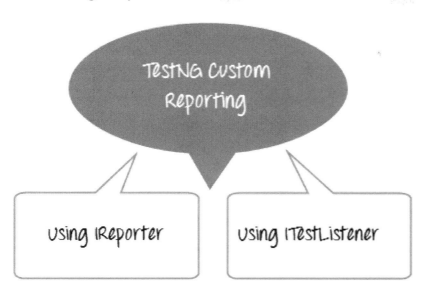

ITestListener Interface

We use this interface when we need to customize real time report. In other words, if we are executing the bunch of test cases in a TetNG suite and we want to get the report of each test case, then after each test case we need to implement ITestListener interface. This interface will override onTestFailure, onTestStart

, onTestSkipped method to send the correct status of the current test case.

Here are the steps we will follow

- Create a class say RealGuru99Report and implement iTestListener in it.
- Implement methods of iTestListener
- Create test method and add RealGuru99Report class as a listener in Test Method class.

```
@Listeners(RealGuru99TimeReport.class)
public class TestGuru99RealReport {

    @Test
```

Code Example

RealGuru99TimeReport.java is the real time reporting class. It will implement ITestListener interface for reporting

```java
package testNGReport.realTimeReport;

import org.testng.ITestContext;

import org.testng.ITestListener;

import org.testng.ITestResult;

public class RealGuru99TimeReport implements ITestListener{

    @Override

    public void onStart(ITestContext arg0) {

        System.out.println("Start Of Execution(TEST)->"+arg0.getName());

    }

    @Override

    public void onTestStart(ITestResult arg0) {

        System.out.println("Test Started->"+arg0.getName());

    }

    @Override

    public void onTestSuccess(ITestResult arg0) {

        System.out.println("Test Pass->"+arg0.getName());

    }
```

```java
    @Override

    public void onTestFailure(ITestResult arg0) {

        System.out.println("Test Failed->"+arg0.getName());

    }

    @Override

    public void onTestSkipped(ITestResult arg0) {

        System.out.println("Test Skipped->"+arg0.getName());

    }

    @Override

    public void onFinish(ITestContext arg0) {

System.out.println("END Of Execution(TEST)->"+arg0.getName());

    }

    @Override

    public void onTestFailedButWithinSuccessPercentage(ITestResult arg0) {

        // TODO Auto-generated method stub



    }



}
```

TestGuru99RealReport.java is the test case for real report

```java
package testNGReport.realTimeReport;

import org.testng.Assert;

import org.testng.annotations.Listeners;

import org.testng.annotations.Test;
```

```
@Listeners(RealGuru99TimeReport.class)

public class TestGuru99RealReport {

    @Test

    public void testRealReportOne(){

        Assert.assertTrue(true);

    }


    @Test

    public void testRealReportTwo(){

        Assert.assertTrue(false);

    }

    //Test case depends on failed testcase= testRealReportTwo

    @Test(dependsOnMethods="testRealReportTwo")

    public void testRealReportThree(){


    }

}
```

The output will look like-

```
public class RealGuru99TimeReport implements ITestListener
    @Override
    public void onStart(ITestContext arg0) {
        System.out.println("Start Of Execution(TEST)->"+
    }
    @Override
    public void onTestStart(ITestResult arg0) {
        System.out.println("Test Started->"+arg0.getName()
    }
    @Override
    public void onTestSuccess(ITestResult arg0) {
        System.out.println("Test Pass->"+arg0.getName());
    }
    @Override
    public void onTestFailure(ITestResult arg0) {
        System.out.println("Test Failed->"+arg0.getName()
    }

    @Override
    public void onTestSkipped(ITestResult arg0) {
        System.out.println("Test Skipped->"+arg0.getName()
    }

    @Override
    public void onFinish(ITestContext arg0) {
        System.out.println("END Of Execution(TEST)->"+arg0
}
```

Real time report in Console

```
Start Of Execution(TEST)->Default
Test Started->testRealReportOne
Test Pass->testRealReportOne
Test Started->testRealReportTwo
Test Failed->testRealReportTwo
Test Skipped->testRealReportThree
END Of Execution(TEST)->Default te:
PASSED: testRealReportOne
FAILED: testRealReportTwo
java.lang.AssertionError: expected
        at org.testng.Assert.fail(
        at org.testng.Assert.failN
```

These reports created in between execution

IReporter Interface

If we want to customize final test report generated by TestNG, we need to implement IReporter interface. This interface has only one method to implement generateReport. This method has all the information of a complete test execution in the List<ISuite>, and we can generate the report using it.

Code Example

Guru99Reporter.java is the file used to customize report

```
package testNGReport.iReporterReport;

import java.util.Collection;

import java.util.Date;

import java.util.List;

import java.util.Map;

import java.util.Set;

import org.testng.IReporter;
```

```java
import org.testng.IResultMap;

import org.testng.ISuite;

import org.testng.ISuiteResult;

import org.testng.ITestContext;

import org.testng.ITestNGMethod;

import org.testng.xml.XmlSuite;

public class Guru99Reporter implements IReporter{

    @Override

    public void generateReport(List<XmlSuite> arg0, List<ISuite> arg1,

        String outputDirectory) {

    // Second parameter of this method ISuite will contain all the suite executed.

    for (ISuite iSuite : arg1) {

     //Get a map of result of a single suite at a time

        Map<String,ISuiteResult> results =    iSuite.getResults();

     //Get the key of the result map

        Set<String> keys = results.keySet();

    //Go to each map value one by one

        for (String key : keys) {

         //The Context object of current result

        ITestContext context = results.get(key).getTestContext();

        //Print Suite detail in Console

         System.out.println("Suite Name->"+context.getName()

                + "::Report output Ditectory->"+context.getOutputDirectory()
```

```java
                    +"::Suite Name->"+ context.getSuite().getName()

            +"::Start Date Time for execution->"+context.getStartDate()

            +"::End Date Time for execution->"+context.getEndDate());



     //Get Map for only failed test cases

    IResultMap resultMap = context.getFailedTests();

    //Get method detail of failed test cases

    Collection<ITestNGMethod> failedMethods = resultMap.getAllMethods();

    //Loop one by one in all failed methods

    System.out.println("--------FAILED TEST CASE---------");

    for (ITestNGMethod iTestNGMethod : failedMethods) {

        //Print failed test cases detail

        System.out.println("TESTCASE NAME->"+iTestNGMethod.getMethodName()

                +"\nDescription->"+iTestNGMethod.getDescription()

                +"\nPriority->"+iTestNGMethod.getPriority()

                +"\n:Date->"+new Date(iTestNGMethod.getDate()));



    }

  }

  }



}
```

}

TestGuru99ForReporter.java is a demo for Custom reporting

```java
package testNGReport.iReporterReport;

import org.testng.Assert;

import org.testng.annotations.Listeners;

import org.testng.annotations.Test;

//Add listener to listen report and write it when testcas finished

@Listeners(value=Guru99Reporter.class)

public class TestGuru99ForReporter {

    @Test(priority=0,description="testReporterOne")

    public void testReporterOne(){

        //Pass test case

        Assert.assertTrue(true);

    }


    @Test(priority=1,description="testReporterTwo")

    public void testReporterTwo(){

        //Fail test case

        Assert.assertTrue(false);

    }

}
```

Output will be like-

```
Suite Name->Default test::Report outp
--------FAILED TEST CASE------
TESTCASE NAME->testReporterTwo
Description->testReporterTwo
Priority->1
:Date->Sat Jun 28 12:30:49 IST 2014
[TestNG] Time taken by testNGReport.i
[TestNG] Time taken by org.testng.rep
[TestNG] Time taken by org.testng.rep
```

Suite Detail

```
estContext context = results.get(key).getTestContext();
Print Suite detail in Console
ystem.out.println("Suite Name->"+context.getName()
    + "::Report output Ditectory->"+context.getOutputDirectory()
    +"::Suite Name->"+ context.getSuite().getName()
    +"::Start Date Time for execution->"+context.getStartDate()
    +"::End Date Time for execution->"+context.getEndDate());
```

Failed Testcase detail

```
//Get Map for only failed test cases
IResultMap resultMap = context.getFailedTests();
//Get method detail of failed test cases
Collection<ITestNGMethod> failedMethods = resultMap.getAllMethods();
//Loop one by one in all failed methods
System.out.println("--------FAILED TEST CASE---------");
```

Reporter detail

```
for (ITestNGMethod iTestNGMethod : failedMethods) {
    //Print failed test cases detail
    System.out.println("TESTCASE NAME->"+iTestNGMethod.getMethodName()
        +"\nDescription->"+iTestNGMethod.getDescription()
        +"\nPriority->"+iTestNGMethod.getPriority()
        +"\n:Date->"+new Date(iTestNGMethod.getDate()));
```

PDF and Email of Reports

The above report implementation is quite simple and clear to get you started with report customization.

But in corporate environment, you will need to create highly customized reports. Here is the scenario we will be dealing with

1. Create Custom Report in PDF form

2. Take Screenshots ONLY on Errors. Link to screenshots in PDF

3. Send Email of the PDF

The PDF report looks like this

Default test TESTNG RESULTS

Wed Jul 02 01:21:11 IST 2014

FAILED TESTS

Class	Method	Time (ms)	Exception
[TestClass name=class test.TestGuru99ForReporter]	testReporterOne	9756	java.lang.AssertionError: expected [true] but found [false]{Screen Shot}
[TestClass name=class test.TestGuru99ForReporter]	testReporterTwo	2810	java.lang.AssertionError: expected [true] but found [false]{Screen Shot}

PASSED TESTS

Class	Method	Time (ms)	Exception
[TestClass	testReporter1Two	3030	

To create pdf report we need a **Java** API **IText**. Download it **here** . There is another custom listener class which is actually implementing this IText jar and creating a pdf report for us. Above figure shows the default format of the PDF report generated. You can customize it

Here is how we will approach this

Step 1) Create a Base Class

Step 2) Customize JypersionListerner.Java (PDF creation code)

Step 3) Create a TestGuru99PDFEmail.java which will execute test cases , create PDF

Step 4) Append code to TestGuru99PDFEmail.java to send PDF report via email

Let's look into these steps

Step 1) Create Base Class

This base class has functions to create WebDriver and Take Screenshot

```
package PDFEmail;

import java.io.File;

import org.apache.commons.io.FileUtils;

import org.openqa.selenium.OutputType;

import org.openqa.selenium.TakesScreenshot;

import org.openqa.selenium.WebDriver;
```

```java
import org.openqa.selenium.firefox.FirefoxDriver;

public class BaseClass {

    static WebDriver driver;

    public static WebDriver getDriver(){

        if(driver==null){


        WebDriver driver ;
         System.setProperty("webdriver.firefox.marionette","C:\\geckodriver.exe");
         driver = new FirefoxDriver();


        }

        return driver;

    }


    /**

     * This function will take screenshot

     * @param webdriver

     * @param fileWithPath

     * @throws Exception

     */

    public static void takeSnapShot(WebDriver webdriver,String fileWithPath) throws
Exception{

        //Convert web driver object to TakeScreenshot

        TakesScreenshot scrShot =((TakesScreenshot)webdriver);

        //Call getScreenshotAs method to create image file
```

```
            File SrcFile=scrShot.getScreenshotAs(OutputType.FILE);

        //Move image file to new destination

        File DestFile=new File(fileWithPath);

        //Copy file at destination

        FileUtils.copyFile(SrcFile, DestFile);



    }

}
```

Step 2) Customize JypersionListener.java

We will stick with the default report format. But we will make 2 customizations

- Adding code to instruct JypersionListener to take screenshot on Error

- Attaching the link of the screenshot take in the PDF report

```
public void onTestFailure(ITestResult result) {
    Log("onTestFailure("+result+")");
    String file = System.getProperty("user.dir")+"\\"+"screenshot"+(new Random().nextInt())+".png";
    try {
        BaseClass.takeSnapShot(BaseClass.getDriver(), file);
    } catch (Exception e) {
        // TODO Auto-generated catch block
        e.printStackTrace();
    }
    if (this.failTable == null) {
        this.failTable = new PdfPTable(new float[]{.3f, .3f, .1f, .3f});
        this.failTable.setTotalWidth(20f);
        Paragraph p = new Paragraph("FAILED TESTS", new Font(Font.TIMES_ROMAN, Font.DEFAULTSIZE, Font.BOLD));
        p.setAlignment(Element.ALIGN_CENTER);
        PdfPCell cell = new PdfPCell(p);
        cell.setColspan(4);
        cell.setBackgroundColor(Color.RED);
```

Add code to attach the screenshot to the PDF report

```
Throwable throwable = result.getThrowable();
if (throwable != null) {
    this.throwableMap.put(new Integer(throwable.hashCode()), throwable);
    this.nbExceptions++;

    Chunk imdb = new Chunk("[SCREEN SHOT]", new Font(Font.TIMES_ROMAN, Font.DEFAULTSIZE, Font.UNDERLINE))
        imdb.setAction(new PdfAction("file:///"+file));
        Paragraph  excep = new Paragraph(
            throwable.toString());
        excep.add(imdb);
```

Step 3) Create a TestGuru99PDFEmail.java which will execute test cases , create PDF

- Here we will add JyperionListener.class as listener

- We will Execute 3 test cases.

- Using Assert.assertTrue we will fail 2 test cases while passing just one.

- Screenshot will be taken for the failed test cases only as per our customizations

```
package PDFEmail;

import java.util.Properties;

import javax.activation.DataHandler;

import javax.activation.DataSource;

import javax.activation.FileDataSource;

import javax.mail.BodyPart;

import javax.mail.Message;

import javax.mail.MessagingException;

import javax.mail.Multipart;

import javax.mail.Session;

import javax.mail.Transport;

import javax.mail.internet.AddressException;

import javax.mail.internet.InternetAddress;

import javax.mail.internet.MimeBodyPart;

import javax.mail.internet.MimeMessage;

import javax.mail.internet.MimeMultipart;

import org.openqa.selenium.WebDriver;

import org.testng.Assert;

import org.testng.annotations.AfterSuite;

import org.testng.annotations.Listeners;

import org.testng.annotations.Test;
```

```java
import reporter.JyperionListener;

//Add listener for pdf report generation

@Listeners(JyperionListener.class)

public class TestGuru99PDFReport extends BaseClass {

    WebDriver driver;

    //Testcase failed so screen shot generate

    @Test

    public void testPDFReportOne(){

        driver = BaseClass.getDriver();

        driver.get("http://google.com");

        Assert.assertTrue(false);

    }


    //Testcase failed so screen shot generate

    @Test

    public void testPDFReporTwo(){

        driver = BaseClass.getDriver();

        driver.get("http:/guru99.com");

        Assert.assertTrue(false);

    }


    //Test test case will be pass, so no screen shot on it
```

```
@Test

public void testPDFReportThree(){

    driver = BaseClass.getDriver();

    driver.get("http://demo.guru99.com");

    Assert.assertTrue(true);

}
```

Step 4) Append code to TestGuru99PDFEmail.java to send PDF report via email

- We will use the annotation @AfterSuite to send email of the PDF report
- We will be sending email using Gmail
- To enable Email, need to import many library files like mail.jar, pop3.jar, smptp.jar, etc
- Before you execute this, do enter the from, to email address and password

```
//After complete execution send pdf report by email

    @AfterSuite

    public void tearDown(){

        sendPDFReportByGMail("FROM@gmail.com", "password", "TO@gmail.com", "PDF Report", "");

        }



    /**

     * Send email using java

     * @param from

     * @param pass

     * @param to

     * @param subject

     * @param body
```

```java
        */

    private static void sendPDFReportByGMail(String from, String pass, String to, String
subject, String body) {

Properties props = System.getProperties();

String host = "smtp.gmail.com";

props.put("mail.smtp.starttls.enable", "true");

props.put("mail.smtp.host", host);

props.put("mail.smtp.user", from);

props.put("mail.smtp.password", pass);

props.put("mail.smtp.port", "587");

props.put("mail.smtp.auth", "true");

Session session = Session.getDefaultInstance(props);

MimeMessage message = new MimeMessage(session);

try {

    //Set from address

message.setFrom(new InternetAddress(from));

message.addRecipient(Message.RecipientType.TO, new InternetAddress(to));

//Set subject

message.setSubject(subject);

message.setText(body);

BodyPart objMessageBodyPart = new MimeBodyPart();

objMessageBodyPart.setText("Please Find The Attached Report File!");

Multipart multipart = new MimeMultipart();
```

```java
multipart.addBodyPart(objMessageBodyPart);

objMessageBodyPart = new MimeBodyPart();

//Set path to the pdf report file

String filename = System.getProperty("user.dir")+"\\Default test.pdf";

//Create data source to attach the file in mail

DataSource source = new FileDataSource(filename);

objMessageBodyPart.setDataHandler(new DataHandler(source));

objMessageBodyPart.setFileName(filename);

multipart.addBodyPart(objMessageBodyPart);

message.setContent(multipart);

Transport transport = session.getTransport("smtp");

transport.connect(host, from, pass);

transport.sendMessage(message, message.getAllRecipients());

transport.close();

}

catch (AddressException ae) {

ae.printStackTrace();

}

catch (MessagingException me) {

me.printStackTrace();

}

}

}
```

Download the complete project here

Note: When we click on the screen shot link in pdf, it shows security dialog. We have to allow this dialog to open pdf.

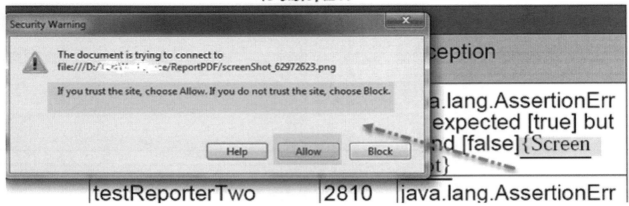

The email so generated will look like this

Summary:

- TestNG has an inbuilt reporting ability in it.

- After a complete execution of test cases, TestNG generates a test-output folder in the root of the project.

- In the test-output folder, there are two main reports, index.html, and emailable-report.html.

- To customize TestNG report we need to implement two interfaces, ITestListener and IReporter.

- If we need to get a report in between execution, we need ITestListener.

- For creating a final report after complete execution, we need to implement IReporter.

- Taking the screenshot, in Selenium WebDriver, we need to type cast WebDriver to TakesScreenShot interface.

- To generate pdf reports we need to add IText jar in the project.

Printed in Great Britain
by Amazon